THE INTERDISCIPLINARY ROOTS
OF GUIDANCE

THE
INTERDISCIPLINARY ROOTS
OF
GUIDANCE

Edited by

THOMAS C. HENNESSY, S.J.

FORDHAM UNIVERSITY PRESS · NEW YORK

Contents

v

Introduction

When the first Chairs of Pedagogy were being established
in the university world at the turn of this century, their
holders were often intent on justifying the professional study
of educational theory and practice as an independent discipline. But nowadays, when schools and departments of education have long since consolidated their positions, even
though they have not appeased their critics, one hears much
more about the need to draw upon a variety of related
disciplines if problems of education are to be properly
examined. Of course, the professional educators would also
maintain that their own adaptations of or experimentation
with the materials borrowed from other fields have resulted
in genuine contributions to these very fields in an authentic
interdisciplinary exchange.

An equally important contribution has been planned in
the development of practical programs for the training of
future teachers. It is now commonly urged that the entire
university be concerned with teacher education and that
specialists from its various departments help prepare people
for this indispensable work. It is not surprising, therefore,

to encounter blueprints for the professional preparation of student guidance counselors which call not only for members of the counselor education staff itself but would also involve such other specialists as the economist, the psychologist, the psychiatrist and the philosopher. This is, to be sure, not only an advanced but a demanding ideal and to enlist the cooperation of many university departments in an enterprise of this sort is not easy. However, the mere recognition of this ideal is itself a sign of progress and one can confidently hope to see it implemented in some institutions in the future.

Two important statements concerning the education of the counselor document this interdisciplinary trend. The report of the Committee on Counselor Education Standards of the Association for Counselor Education and Supervision (January, 1964) devotes one section to prophesying thus about the adequate university of the future: "Cooperation exists between staff members directly responsible for the professional education of counselors and representatives of departments or schools offering courses in related schools." Furthermore, these representatives of related disciplines will become involved in the "curriculum planning, implementation and evaluation" of the counselor education program.

The Division of Counseling Psychology of the American Psychological Association has also produced its own Scope and Standards of Preparation in Psychology for School Counselors (1962). This document maintains that the education of the counselor "should be interdisciplinary in nature." It continues: "Each discipline should be taught by qualified specialists trained in the discipline itself and oriented to the work of the counselor."

In July, 1964 a step was taken toward translating these forecasts and recommendations into practice at the Eighth Annual Guidance Institute conducted by the Division of Educational Psychology, Measurements and Guidance of the School of Education of Fordham University. The papers collected in this volume were originally prepared for this institute.

It seems appropriate to indicate the thinking behind the choice of the disciplines represented in the papers. At the same time, the nexus between the papers can be shown.

The economist discusses certain basic realities upon which many of the choices in life are founded, particularly the opportunities which are available for employment. The economist also educates the counselor to the need for alertness to the coming changes in occupational fields. The psychiatrist, speaking from another perspective, stresses the fact that man has certain inner needs which must be acknowledged and provided for, regardless of surrounding circumstances. The psychiatrist and the psychologist have contributed toward a knowledge of these inner needs through improved interview techniques and through batteries of tests of different kinds. In addition, the psychologist has a good deal to say about vocational development in light of the fulfillment of personal needs during the series of choices which precede stability in a given career. While the psychologist views his client's values as an important element in his personality structure, the sociologist and anthropologist concentrate much of their attention on the values of the individual and the group. The guidance counselor and the social worker use the findings of all these disciplines in their work of helping and understanding the person. The counselor, however, tends to devote his time to the "normal" person, while the social worker offers his services to those whose behavior is regarded as abnormal.

At times the interdisciplinary approach is concluded with the examination of the contributions of the scientific and applied behavioral sciences. However, guidance ideally owes and should express its debt to two other major disciplines: philosophy and theology. Both of them provide concepts about the nature of man. Philosophy investigates man, his needs, values and aspirations, in the light of human reason and wisdom. It recognizes that a fundamental problem for each man is the reality of his personal freedom. Theology, on the other hand, looks at man with the help of Biblical sources and its own traditions. The modern theologian shows the integration between his area and the data offered by other specialists. For instance, it is possible for the theologian to acknowledge certain needs of which psychiatrists and psychologists speak and then show how these are satisfied through the teachings and practices of religion.

Literature and history, though not presented in the papers in this book, should also be mentioned as sources of help in the field of guidance. In both disciplines, as in theology, the example of outstanding human figures has helped many a youth in his quest for the meaning and goals of life. Youth identifies with many of these persons and absorbs ideals and ideas from their words and works. How many a youth of the 1960s has been inspired to public service both at home and abroad because of the example and urging of John Fitzgerald Kennedy. Dr. Thomas Dooley performed a like service in our own generation. In the past our national heroes (Washington, Lincoln, Lee) and the heroes of all nations exerted a similar influence.

There is another subject to which the guidance practitioner must give more than token attention and more than passing acknowledgment. That is statistics. Through the methods provided by statistics, the guidance counselor is enabled to study the group and the individual. He can learn with assurance the levels of the group, the norm, and the differential aspects of each person with whom he deals. He can ascertain true rather than apparent differences in data concerning individuals. With the instruments which the statistician makes available, he can even engage in some general predictions concerning the individual's likelihood of success in a college or occupation.

Though suggestions were made to the lecturers, each of them freely chose the aspect of their specialty which seemed most appropriate to him. One could perhaps dispute certain emphases and the neglect of other aspects of their discipline. However, each has opened up wide and important vistas for consideration and evaluation. To do adequate justice to each of the disciplines a separate book would be required for the eight areas. Perhaps an enterprising scholar or publisher will sponsor such a series. In the meantime, we hope that the readers of these papers will find them as rewarding as did the members of the 1964 Institute when they were first delivered.

Louis F. Buckley

is the New York Regional Administrator, Bureau of Employment Security, U.S. Department of Labor. Before holding his present position, he had been the New York Regional Director, U.S. Bureau of Labor Statistics. He received his A.B. and M.A. degrees at Notre Dame University and did additional graduate work in economics at Illinois University, the University of Wisconsin and Catholic University. He has taught at Notre Dame, Western Reserve, Loyola (Chicago) and Fordham universities. He is a member of the Mayor's Committee on Exploitation of Workers and the Mayor's Committee on Youth and Work in New York City. His published articles include: "The Migrant Worker Today," "1960 Manpower Trends and Automation's Impact," "The Changing Composition of our Labor Force," and "College Women and the Labor Market."

Economics and Guidance

Margaret Mead has observed that "we have a right to demand that guidance workers draw effectively upon all that the modern life sciences can give them." It is significant that economics is represented in this book as a related discipline in addition to five of the behavioral sciences, as well as philosophy and theology. Economics as a base for counseling has been strangely neglected. Gilbert Wrenn, in a study made for the American Personnel and Guidance Association, observed that the school counselor cannot afford to be a graduate student in psychology and a second grader in economics (Wrenn, p. 42). Since voca-

1

tional choice in our democratic society is free, within the limits of certain determining factors, those who are in a position to influence vocational choice occupy a special position in relation to the economic system. The more specialized the society, the more important the guidance function (Overs, p. 213).

The origin of vocational guidance in the early years of the present century has been traced to the problems arising from the industrial revolution with its creation of new and specialized occupations in contrast to the agricultural era where the son followed in the occupation of his father. The resulting confusion, uncertainty, insecurity, and readjustment, according to Harold Goldstein, "cried out for some form of order in the chaos and, in our rational, pragmatic society, vocational guidance was the inevitable answer" (Goldstein, p. 227).

The economic revolution, which we are now experiencing, is likely to change the occupational structure more drastically than did the industrial revolution. The year 1950 is often referred to as the break between the period of rapid change and that of radical change. What is different now is the pace of change. David Sarnoff of RCA predicts that science and technology will advance more in the next thirty-six years than in all the millennia since man's creation.

THE LABOR MARKET

I would like to center my attention on the labor market aspects of economics which are of particular significance to the counselor. Emphasis will be placed on the important changes which are taking place in the demand for and the supply of labor which are indicative of what we may expect in the future. The following thought from Abraham Lincoln might be considered as a text for this approach: "If we could first know where we are and whither we are tending, we could better judge what to do and how to do it."

2

CHANGES IN INDUSTRY

The nature of the demand for labor has changed in many respects during the past fifteen years. Within the overall pattern of increase in demand for labor, some industries, like agriculture and mining, have shown a steady decline. Demand for labor in contract construction grew at a rapid pace during the first decade of the postwar period, but has changed very little in the past several years. In the largest industry sector—manufacturing—the demand for labor has had wide fluctuations between industries without a discernible overall trend of increase or decline.

A significant change in demand for labor took place about 1950, when, for the first time in history, the number of workers in service industries, which include trade, transportation, public utilities, finance, insurance, real estate, government and other services, surpassed the number in the production or goods-producing industries, which include manufacturing, agriculture, construction and mining. The proportion of all workers in goods-producing industries declined from 51 percent in 1947 to 46 percent in 1957, and fell to about 40 percent in 1963. The rate of decline in the proportion of goods-producing employment in the economy in the last six years has been almost two times greater than in the previous decade. The United States is the only country in the world in which the jobs in services outnumber the jobs in goods industries.

The principal reason why the demand for the majority of our workers is in the service-producing sectors of the American economy is because of the extraordinary increases which have taken place in output per man hour in the goods-producing industries. As a result, we simply need fewer people to put out the enormous complex of goods that we have available to us. Underlying the productivity gains are a number of factors, including technological advances, improvements in the quality of the labor force, increases in capital investment, and investments in research and development.

The major buying sectors which determine the demand for

3

goods and services and the ultimate demand for labor are individual consumers, business, government and export. Purchases by government have shown a far greater tendency to rise over the last several decades than those by other sectors. Wars, international tensions, and depressions, along with population growth, have all provided the impetus at one time or another to increase purchases by government agencies—federal, state and local. During the postwar period the trend continued, with government expenditures more than doubling in real terms. Although there has been a substantial slackening in the rate of growth of federal purchases since 1957, state and local spending continued their steady rise resulting from increased demands for community services mainly related to population growth and the critical problem of expanding urban communities. Gains in employment have been especially rapid in education, health and hospital and sanitation services.

Purchases by individuals, which have grown steadily, account for the largest share of national demand for goods and services. However, outlays for services showed the most persistent increase. Families tend to spend relatively less of their income for goods, such as food, but more for health and recreation, housing, transportation and financial services. Expenditures on business plant and equipment and on residential construction have varied widely. While investment spending is much smaller in total volume than consumer expenditures, the role of investment is crucial to increased labor force productivity.

OCCUPATIONAL CHANGE

The changes in labor demands, from the viewpoint of industries which we have discussed, are reflected in changing occupational demands for labor. The divergent industry employment trends have brought with them, inevitably, marked changes in the demand for workers in different occupations. The decrease in the demand for farmers and farm labor which was part and parcel of the overall decline in agricultural employment is an obvious illustration. In addition, the emergence of new indus-

4

tries (television and atomic energy, for example) has given rise to wholly new occupations.

Within industries, the occupational composition of the work force has been affected by a great variety of factors, of which the most pervasive is technological change. As a result of technological innovations, new occupations have emerged while others have expanded, contracted or even disappeared. The new *Dictionary of Occupational Titles* will contain about 22,000 jobs of which 6,000 will be new to the Dictionary. Many of these new jobs are also relatively new in the economy.

A shift in employment toward white-collar occupations (professional, managerial, clerical and sales) and a relative decline in blue-collar groups (craftsmen, operatives, and laborers) has been evident since the beginning of the century. In 1956, for the first time in our history, professional, managerial, clerical, and sales employees outnumbered employees in manual occupations. These trends reflect the increased demand in service industries where more white-collar workers are employed and the slower employment growth in goods-producing industries which have relatively large numbers of blue-collar jobs.

In addition to the workers in white-collar and blue-collar occupations, there are two broad occupational groups—farm and service workers—which do not fit neatly into either category because they include workers of both types. The persistent decline in employment of farm workers has been interrupted in only three of the fifteen postwar years. Employment of service workers, on the other hand, has increased notably. In 1953, for the first time, the number of workers employed in service occupations— cooks, janitors, barbers, etc.—exceeded that of farm workers, and the differences have widened fairly steadily since then— providing one more indication of the shift in employment from goods-oriented jobs to service-oriented jobs in our economy.

The fastest growing demand for occupational groups during the decade 1950 to 1960 was for professional, technical and kindred workers. This group includes all the recognized professions—teaching, engineering, law, the ministry, the various health professions, the natural and social sciences, and many

5

others. It also includes a large number of technical and kindred occupations—for example, the many types of technicians who work with engineers and scientists and with members of the health professions. Such occupations typically require less education than is needed for fully professional work, although many experienced technicians have jobs demanding considerable technical training.

Employment demand for professional and technical workers as a group increased by 47 percent between 1950 and 1960—a rate of growth more than three times the average for all occupational groups. However, employment demand grew much faster for some professions than others. The number of engineers, for example, increased by about 64 percent over the decade; among engineers, the aeronautical group grew fastest, increasing by 193 percent.

Although there has been a decline in the number of self-employed proprietors, the number of managers and other salaried officials required by private industry and government increased by more than a third during the past decade. Clerical workers increased 34 percent between 1950 and 1960. Despite the strides made in the automation of many clerical functions, the demand for certain types of clerical workers has continued to rise—due partly to the substantial expansion of industries such as finance, insurance and government. Demand for secretaries and typists increased about 70 percent during the 1950s. Other clerical occupations showing rapid increases in demand were office machine operators, receptionists, cashiers, and bank tellers. The number of workers required in wholesale trade and other industries increased by 33 percent in contrast to only a 10 percent increase in retail trade.

Turning now to the demand for blue-collar workers, we find only an increase of 12 percent in the 1950s. More than two-thirds of the increase occurred among foremen, mechanics and repairmen. Construction craftsmen, who constitute one-fourth of all skilled workers, had only a small increase in employment over the decade. Skilled workers who decreased in numbers during the decade included locomotive firemen and engineers, railroad mechanics, furriers, jewelers and shoemakers. The operative or semi-skilled group as a whole did not change significantly in absolute numbers during the 1950's. Machines have been substituted for the more routinized operations performed by semi-skilled workers. Such changes have permitted great expansion in production without commensurate increases in the demand for machine operators. Demand for drivers and deliverymen rose by almost 20 percent between 1950 and 1960.

Another major effect of changing technology has been the declining need for industrial laborers. Employment in laboring jobs dropped by almost 10 percent between 1950 and 1960. Requirements for laborers have decreased primarily because of the increasing substitution of machinery for unskilled labor in the handling and moving of heavy objects, in unloading and in excavating. In contrast, demand for service workers has increased almost twice as fast as employment generally during the 1950-60 period. The increase in employment of hospital attendants and practical nurses was very sizable. Other types of service workers who had substantial increases in employment were waiters, cooks and counter workers in restaurants.

GEOGRAPHIC TRENDS

The shifts in the industrial demand for manpower which we have discussed have also contributed to changes in the location of employment. The older industrial areas of the Northeast and Great Lakes have grown at a much slower pace than the nation as a whole, while the southern and western regions experienced a much faster growth. In California, Oregon and Washington, employment rose 61 percent in the past 15 years. Along the South Atlantic coast it increased by 41 percent. In contrast, employment in New England rose by only 13 percent and actually declined in West Virginia and Rhode Island.

7

EMPLOYMENT OF WOMEN

The greatly increased demand for women in the labor market has been a most striking recent development and reflects the trend toward white-collar occupations and the expansion of industries which normally employ a large number of women, such as trade. The greatest increase in demand for women has been in the professional group where 58 percent more women were employed in 1962 than in 1950. Teaching is the largest occupational group in the professional employment of women. There have been increases of over 50 percent also in the employment of women in clerical work and as service workers such as waitresses. About 30 percent of women workers are employed part-time. The demand for part-time workers exists most frequently among private-household workers, sales workers and waitresses.

NEGRO EMPLOYMENT

There have been increases in the demand for Negro workers in some of the professional, technical and clerical fields and in other white-collar occupations. The largest relative gains made by Negroes between 1955-62 were in professional services, such as hospital, medical, and other services, and in welfare and religious institutions. Negroes also have experienced relatively sharp gains in the growing fields of educational services and public administration. Howard University recently reported that 319 companies had visited their campus in 1964 recruiting their graduates. This is an increase of 300 over 1963. A recent report by the President's Equal Employment Opportunity Committee, based on data from 4610 companies with a total of 2,404,253 employees, indicated that white-collar employment of Negroes increased 17.4 percent from 1962 to 1963 while total employment in these occupations rose by only 1.9 percent. The Negroes started from so small a base, however, that the gain increased their percentage of total white-collar employment in the companies from 1.2 percent to only 1.3 percent.

Despite this limited progress in the shift of the Negro to white-collar and skilled occupations, it must be recognized that in 1962 only 17 percent of all employed Negroes were in white-collar occupations, compared with 47 percent of white workers. White workers in this group outnumbered Negroes 28 to 1, in marked contrast to their comparative representation in the civilian labor force (10 white for each Negro worker). Unless there is a substantial acceleration of the trends noted, the percentage of Negro workers in white-collar employment will be substantially below that of white workers for many years. The rate of increase in Negro employment in the white-collar occupations must be expedited as these are the occupations which will show the greatest rate of growth in the future.

The future is even bleaker than the present for the Negro worker in many respects because the gap is widening between the occupational distribution of Negro workers and the nature of the demand for workers in the labor market. Forty-three percent of Negroes compared to 25 percent of white workers are in semi-skilled or unskilled occupations. These jobs tend to be concentrated in those goods-producing and related industries which are quite sensitive to the business cycle. Moreover, the demand for this type of labor has diminished steadily during the postwar period as a result of automation and other technological developments. On the other hand, less than 10.0 percent of Negro workers compared to over 30 percent of white workers are employed in professional, technical, managerial and sales occupations where the demand for workers is expanding.

RISING EDUCATIONAL REQUIREMENTS

The most rapidly expanding occupations, professional, technical, managerial, clerical and skilled, are those which require the most education and training. The average years of school completed by those in the professional and technical occupations now exceed four years of college and in clerical and sales they exceed four years of high school. A high school diploma is generally required now for entrance into skilled jobs and to an

9

increasing extent even in the operative occupations. As Secretary of Labor, Willard Wirtz, has stated: "The machines now have, in general, a high school education—in the sense that they can do most jobs that a high school education qualifies people to do. So machines will get the unskilled jobs, because they work for less than living wages. Machines are, in the most real sense, responsible for putting uneducated people out of work."

SUPPLY OF MANPOWER

The growth in the country's labor force over the past two decades has been very substantial. From 56 million in 1940, the number of workers grew to 73 million in 1960. This gain of 17 million workers was the largest ever experienced in this country in any 20-year period. Between 1957 and 1962, the net annual increase in the labor force averaged about three-quarters of a million. In 1963, with improved employment conditions and with the first large group of the postwar baby boom reaching working age, the labor force rose sharply by 1.1 million.

Women have accounted for about three-fifths of the entire labor force increase over the 1947-62 period. This recent rise in women's employment has occurred almost entirely among married women. For women, labor force participation reaches a peak in the late teens and early twenties, as they leave school, and then drops in the middle twenties as marriage and motherhood bring withdrawals from the work force. After they reach 35 or thereabouts and their children reach school age, the proportion employed outside the home rises. It reaches a new peak at ages 45 to 54 and then tends to drop off, since many women stop working at a younger age than is customary for men.

A substantial rise in the educational attainment of American workers has been achieved. The relative numbers of workers who are college graduates have risen especially fast in the past 10 years—from 7.9 percent in 1952 to 11 percent in 1962, for those 18 years old and over. The increase in the proportions that have had at least a high school education is also noteworthy. This proportion rose from 42.8 to 53.8 percent over the past decade, a gain of more than 25 percent. At the lower end of the educational ladder, the proportion of workers with less than 5 years of school fell from 7.3 to 4.6 percent.

IMBALANCE IN THE LABOR MARKET

Maladjustments in the forces of supply and demand in the labor market have resulted in a serious and persistent problem of unemployment. Despite a lengthy period of expansion in economic activity, the 1962-63 unemployment rates stubbornly remained between 5½ and 6 percent. The year 1963 marked the sixth consecutive year in which unemployment rates failed to return to the 4 percent level which prevailed during most of the 1955-57 period. Moreover, the trend in unemployment has been getting progressively worse. In each of the last few business booms, the unemployment rate has failed to decline to a level as low as that reached at the peak of the previous expansion. The unemployment rate for non-white workers is more than double that of white workers.

Teenage unemployment rose in 1963. An average of nearly 1 million teenage boys and girls were unemployed in 1963, compared with 800,000 during 1962. At 15½ percent, the 1963 teenage unemployment rate was close to those recorded in the recession years of 1958 and 1961, and higher than in any other postwar year.

About 1.1 million or 26 percent of the unemployed in 1963 had been seeking work 15 weeks or longer. In terms of skill levels, unskilled workers, service workers and semi-skilled operatives together represented more than three-fifths of the experienced unemployed in 1963, while they accounted for only two-fifths of all employed persons.

A major factor which accounts for the imbalance in the labor market, thus resulting in unemployment, is that the great increase in demand for labor has been concentrated in occupations at the top of the ladder in terms of education and skill at a time when there is not a sufficient supply of labor available to meet the qualifications of the so-called "knowledge" occupations. And

11

even in occupations where the supply of workers may approximate the demand on a nationwide basis, local shortages can and do develop, owing to sudden increases in local demand, to lack of worker mobility, and to other frictions and inefficiencies in the operation of the labor market.

Other important factors which explain imbalance include the inability of the labor demand growth to absorb the increases taking place in labor supply and the workers displaced because of technological improvements. These two factors alone—labor force and productivity increase—required a growth in employment opportunities equivalent to about 3 million jobs between 1962 and 1963 if a rise in unemployment was to be prevented. Unfortunately this amount of growth was not achieved in 1963 or in recent years.

The major industrial and occupational changes during the past fifteen years which we have discussed are likely to continue during the next ten years. We may expect a continuation of the more rapid growth of the so-called white-collar group of occupations, a smaller growth in the blue-collar occupations and a faster-than-average growth among service workers and a further decline among farmers and farm laborers. The direction of employment demand is clearly for workers with more education and greater skill. The occupational outlook also is assuming an increasingly international aspect. More people will have jobs abroad in the next decade. An uncertain element on the demand side of the labor market is the possible decrease in the defense budget which accounts for expenditures of $51 billion dollars a year. We are now feeling the effect of the recent decrease in this budget.

The dramatic technological developments which we have witnessed during the past fifteen years are but the beginning of fundamental, industrial and occupational changes which will continue at an accelerating rate as far ahead as we can see. The application of this new technology will extend outside the factory and major industries will probably develop that do not exist now as was the case of computer production in the last fifteen years.

Demand created by replacement needs is of equal importance to net employment growth. In fact, the number of persons who will be required to replace workers who retire, die or leave the work force for other reasons between 1960 and 1970 will exceed the 13.8 million net growth in employment projected for the economy as a whole during that period.

Another aspect of impending manpower adjustment relates to changes in the pattern of labor supply stemming from growth in the labor force. During the next twelve months 1 million more young people will be reaching age 18 than in the last twelve months, or an increase of over 35 percent. This large growth results from a sharp increase in the birth rate during the postwar period. Although fortunately a large number of these young people will not enter the labor market until later, the number of new young workers entering the labor force annually will increase from two million in 1960 to three million in 1970. This increase represents a far greater number than the economy has ever had to absorb in a single decade.

The sheer number of workers who will be entering the labor force to seek work next year and in the years immediately ahead represents only one aspect of the problem. The adequacy of their education and training to meet the rising job requirements of a fast growing economy reflects another of the problem's dimensions.

LABOR MARKET IMPLICATIONS FOR GUIDANCE

The changing industrial and occupational structure, the changing geography of American industry, the changing educational prerequisites of employment and the changing size and educational attainment of the work force which we have discussed are major factors with which the counselor must cope. These changes should be considered a prelude to even more rapid and extensive change which we must anticipate in the future. Seymour L. Wolfbein of the U.S. Department of Labor emphasizes that change will continue to be a surpassingly important dimension in the field of counseling. He has redefined the concept of the education and guidance process as helping the individual to withstand the onslaughts and, in fact to take advantage of the inevitable changes which will occur in the world of work (Borow, p. 171).

The counselor must recognize that safe and secure occupations of the present may be obsolete in the future. Margaret Mead has observed, "No one will live all his life in the world in which he was born, and no one will die in the world in which he worked at maturity." This situation emphasizes the need to look at long-run employment prospects rather than at the immediate situation in career planning. It indicates that overemphasis on specific skills should be avoided at the expense of developing basic capabilities. Those preparing to enter the world of work must acquire a broad-based background which will equip them with maximum ability to adjust to change. John Diebold, head of a consulting firm, and a recognized authority on automation, maintains that counselors should no longer emphasize the choice of one career as a lifetime pursuit (Diebold, p. 1). Young people must also recognize that additional education throughout adult life will be increasingly necessary as occupational skills need constant refurbishing. Similarly, guidance must be considered to be a developmental process over the lifetime of the individual.

Louis Levine, Director, United States Employment Service stresses that "employment counselors must consciously and deliberately think in terms of change. They must think in terms of long-range projections and must adopt an attitude of anticipation of a preparation for change. They must think 'future' and keep abreast of information on new job fields, or they will be counseling for a world of work that no longer exists."

IDENTIFICATION AND CULTIVATION OF TALENT

The counselor can make an important contribution toward reducing the imbalance between the abilities of our labor force and the labor demand requirements of the new technology which we have discussed. By 1970, the experts predict industry and government will have a deficit of at least 20,000 physicists—about one-third of the total number required. The Engineering Manpower Commission of the Engineers Joint Council cited with alarm the increasing advantage the Soviet Union is establishing in the production of engineers. It noted that the Russians are outproducing the United States better than 3 to 1. During 1961, the Red Chinese turned out 19,000 engineers—five times as many as in 1950. In the same period, engineering graduates in this country declined from 42,000 to 36,000. As individuals and as a nation we are engaged in a competitive struggle to maintain a position of world leadership. Albert S. Thompson of Columbia University points out that "just as the passing of the frontier in the late 1800s meant that we could no longer be so profligate with our natural resources, so the current challenge to our world leadership in social and technical developments means that we cannot afford to waste our human resources" (Borow, p. 488).

The counselor can play an increasing role in identifying individuals with rare and exceptional talent and in helping these individuals analyze their abilities and aptitudes in order to determine which of these abilities can be utilized to the best advantage. The counselor also has a function in the cultivation of talent as the student must have opportunities to acquire the education and training appropriate for him and also he must have the desire to do so.

THE POTENTIAL DROPOUT

Since our analysis has indicated that most of the expanding job opportunities require an educational background, it is essential that more of our young people are motivated to remain in school. The extent to which school dropouts find difficulty in fitting into the labor market is indicated in that the rate of unemployment for 1962 school dropouts in October was 29 percent, about twice as high as the rate for the June high school graduates despite the higher proportion of dropouts in farm areas, where unemployment is less common. The situation for dropouts can be expected to worsen in the coming years, because little growth or some declines are expected in occupations with low educational and skill requirements and workers without at least a high school diploma will have increasing difficulty entering expanding occupations where educational and training qualifications are high. They will constitute a new disadvantaged minority group in the American labor force—increasingly handicapped in competing for jobs because of the greater availability of graduates and decreasing opportunities for partly-educated workers.

Seymour Wolfbein, of the U.S. Department of Labor, has pointed out that many, if not most, of our potential dropouts have neither the predilection nor the aptitude for academic, college-preparatory courses of training. But a very large group is composed of manually–talented boys for whom meaningful courses of instruction in the vocational area would make the difference between dropping out of school and achieving a high school diploma. This is an opportunity to build meaningful pathways which will help the young person realize his potential and at the same time help fill our needs for skilled personnel.

THE SKILLED WORKER

As an increasing proportion of the brighter than average young people go on to college, as the percentage rises from one-fourth to one-third of our population, we are running the risk of starving the skilled and service occupations of competent workers. We have seen that among blue-collar workers, the craftsmen, foremen and kindred workers will continue to have the most favorable employment outlook. Because of the mounting need for mechanics and repairmen to install and maintain the ever-increasing amount of complex equipment used by industry, government agencies and private households, employment of these workers will continue to increase rapidly.

It is of major importance that guidance and counseling personnel familiarize themselves with the need for skilled workers. It is important for them to know and impart the fact that the crafts represent one of the best fields for young persons. These occupations rank near the top of the earning scale. About three out of every four who are employed are year-round full-time workers. They enjoy greater-than-average job security. Their unemployment rate is only half that of the unskilled workers.

It is essential that all of us help to endow the craftsman with the stature and status he deserves. Seymour Wolfbein has observed that too often, the young person pursuing a non-academic course, preparing himself for a trade, is considered to be at the bottom of the totem pole, down in the ranks of the untalented. This is an entirely false impression. The skills and aptitudes may be different from those of professional or other personnel, but they can be just as difficult to acquire, just as complex in their concepts and techniques, and they are just as strategic to the growth of our economy.

GUIDANCE OF SPECIAL GROUPS

The counselor must assume an increasing role in the war on poverty by providing disadvantaged groups of young people with the guidance needed to assist them in preparing themselves for a place in the complicated and changing labor market we have discussed. Young people who come from low-income families and suffer from social deprivations must be given special consideration and attention by the counselor. The report of the Senate Committee on Labor and Public Welfare in considering amendments to the Manpower Development and Training Act summarized this problem as follows: "Dropouts leave school for many reasons not necessarily related to their intellectual capacity or potential. Their reasons are rooted in the poverty, discrimina-

17

tion, and social chaos in which they have been reared. Their motivation has been corroded by a hostile society."

Unless we are more successful in making young people appreciate that the lack of a high school diploma is rapidly becoming an impassable barrier to entrance into the labor force and to stable employment and unless we succeed in motivating young people to complete their education, we are committing them to economic suicide. Secretary of Labor Willard Wirtz expanded on this matter recently when he said the nation is stacking up young boys and girls just out of school on an economic slag heap at a rate of a quarter of a million a year.

The current Negro situation would not be so serious if all of us, educators, counselors and the public, had done a better job of preparing young Negroes for the shortage occupations in the professional and technical fields which are opening to them today. The National Urban League did outstanding pioneer work in this area by encouraging, motivating, and assisting young Negroes to obtain the kind of education needed for work in the technical and scientific fields while many counselors were thinking in terms of continued entrance of Negroes only in the unskilled and least desirable service occupations where they formerly could find work.

Another group that requires special mention are girls. Our analysis of labor market trends indicates that nine out of ten women are likely to work outside of their home during the course of their lives. An increasing number of women will make significant contributions in vocations in the world of work as well as in the home as wife and mother. This is another situation where the counselor has contributed to the restrictive concept of limited occupational choice because they are women.

There is need for particular emphasis on the counseling of talented girls. Because of the current pattern of early marriage, many girls take it for granted that they will work for only a few years at most, and so fail to take seriously their educational and vocational planning. Yet, as indicated earlier in our analysis, women in their 30s are going to work in rising numbers after their children reach school age. By helping girls to realize that they may spend many years at work, even if they marry, and assisting them to plan their education accordingly, counselors can contribute to the later job satisfaction and income of many women. If you can stimulate bright girls to think more seriously about their professional potentialities, you may also help to relieve the national shortage of creative personnel.

An interesting by-product of the education of women is that studies of college students indicate a closer relationship between the education of the mother and college attendance than does the education of the father. As one author commented, this might make those persons think who contend it more important to educate our men than our women. Evidently, one of the ways to obtain more educated men is to have more educated mothers (Berdie, p. 462).

OCCUPATIONAL INFORMATION

Counselors, in order to give meaningful guidance, must keep abreast of the rapidly changing world of work. They must be able to help young people acquire an accurate picture of the hard facts of the American job market in relation to their interests, aptitudes and abilities, that they may be better able to make an intelligent choice of occupational goals.

I am sure you are familiar with the basic occupational information available in the following Department of Labor publications: *Occupational Outlook Handbook, Occupational Outlook Quarterly, Job Guide for Young Workers* and *Dictionary of Occupational Titles.* Many state public employment services have occupational guides and area skill surveys available in localities which are helpful in becoming better acquainted with local labor market conditions.

Annual reports are required under the Manpower Development and Training Act of 1962, on manpower requirements, resources, utilization and training. I relied on these reports issued in March, 1963 and 1964 for much of the basic information used in my analysis of the labor market in this discussion. There are other developments which will assure us of even more comprehensive and adequate occupational information. Under the Manpower Development and Training Act, local public employment agencies must determine whether or not manpower shortages exist and the probable opportunity for placement of trainees in various occupations. Furthermore, the Vocational Education Act of 1963 places the responsibility upon state public employment agencies to inform the State Board of Education about job opportunities and job requirements for which training is needed. In carrying out this assignment, public employment services are directed to collect information not otherwise available about jobs in fields of work for which vocational training is deemed practicable.

I would urge that the interdisciplinary approach which is stressed in this book be followed by counselors in establishing working relations with the agencies in the community which can assist in keeping the school counselor familiar with the present and future employment needs of the community. Such information and working arrangements should include in addition to the local state employment office, groups representing employers, labor unions, religious organizations and professional organizations. In areas where local manpower committees have been formed to advise the state employment service, counselors may want to discuss with the local committee chairmen their need for being advised of current labor market developments.

All individuals planning to leave school should be made aware of services provided by state employment offices. School guidance personnel should take advantage of the referral, testing, vocational counseling, and placement services provided by state employment offices for both part-time summer opportunities and for entry job placement. Cooperative arrangements have been developed in many communities whereby potential dropouts, particularly those without definite job prospects, are referred to the local public employment office prior to actually leaving school.

I was impressed during a visit to Germany with the practice followed there of having attractive calendars in each classroom which carry pictures of various occupations. Time is spent each week discussing one of the occupations so that students at an early age obtain a knowledge of the nature and requirements of the jobs. Emphasis is placed on every type of occupation including, in particular, the manual or blue-collar jobs. I believe we could do much more and begin at an early age (grade school) in this country to develop an interest and to provide information which will be helpful to the student when he is ready to make a vocational choice. It must be recognized that vocational choice and adjustment is a long-time process which is never completely finished.

I also liked the emphasis placed by counselors in Germany on meeting with parents to discuss vocational choice. A program of this nature might serve a purpose in this country in dealing with parents who fail to provide children with the proper incentive for achievement. It might also serve to deter parents who drive their children into academic programs beyond their abilities and thus into failure and frustration.

CONCLUSION

That the need for guidance and counseling services will mount sharply in the years ahead and will assume a greater, more important and more decisive role is one of the findings which emerges most clearly from our analysis of our rapidly changing occupational structure. Counselors will be called upon to guide unprecedented numbers of young people in a vocational adjustment likely to present difficult problems. Moreover, the vocational aspects of counseling including the providing of occupational information, are likely to assume steadily increasing importance in view of the competition for available jobs and the shifts in occupational requirements which will occur in this period of rapid technological change.

Our democracy is now engaged in a world-wide struggle with a totalitarian system, in which the government can direct the education and training of the people in a manner designed to achieve an allocation among occupations in accordance with its concept of national needs. In our country, we face the much more difficult task of meeting the nation's needs for specialized personnel without impairing freedom of choice for the individual.

What is needed and is evolving to meet this challenge is the cooperation and the effective working relationships of all groups who have any bearing on education, counseling, training, employment and the job market process. The pattern of cooperation is similar to the interdisciplinary approach being used so effectively in this book. Each discipline and each interested group will contribute its special training and background to work as an effective team in achieving a solution to these challenging manpower problems based on the total acceptance of the dignity and worth of each individual as a human being.

REFERENCES

Berdie, Ralph F. The counselor and his manpower responsibilities. *The Personnel and Guidance Journal,* February, 1960, 458-463.

Borow, Henry (ed.). *Man in a world at work.* Boston: Houghton Mifflin, 1964.

Diebold, John. Automation: its implications for counseling. *Occupational Outlook Quarterly, 6,* No. 3, September, 1962, 1-3.

Goldstein, Harold. Economic setting for vocational guidance. *The Vocational Guidance Quarterly, 11,* No. 4, Summer, 1963, 227-231.

Overs, Robert P. The interaction of vocational counseling with the economic system. *The American Journal of Economics and Sociology, 23,* April, 1964, No. 2, pp. 213-221.

President of the United States. Manpower report of the President and a report on manpower requirements, resources, utilization and training. Washington, D.C.: Government Printing Office, 1963 and 1964.

U.S. Department of Labor. *Manpower Challenge of the 1960s.* Washington, D.C.: Government Printing Office, 1960.

Wood, Helen. The manpower future—its challenge for vocational guidance. *The Personnel and Guidance Journal,* December, 1959, 300-304.

Wrenn, C. Gilbert. *The counselor in a changing world.* Washington, D.C.: American Personnel and Guidance Association, 1962.

ADDITIONAL READING

Baer, M., and Roeber, E. *Occupational information.* Chicago: Science Research, 1963 (rev. ed.).
Buckingham, W. *Automation: its impact on business and people.* New York: Harper, 1961.
Dubin, R. *The world of work.* Englewood Cliffs, N.J.: Prentice Hall, 1958.
Forrester, Gertrude. *Occupational literature.* New York: Wilson, 1964.
George, F. H. *Automation, cybernetics and society.* New York: Philosophical Library, 1959.
Hoppoch, R. *Occupational information.* New York: McGraw-Hill, 1963 (2nd ed.).
Hughes, E. C. *Men and their work.* Glencoe, Ill.: Free Press, 1958.
Jaffe, A. J. *Occupational mobility in the United States, 1930-1960.* New York: Columbia Univ. Press, 1964.
Lauterbach, A. T. *Man, motives and money; psychological frontiers of economics.* Ithaca, N.Y.: Cornell Univ. Press, 1954.
Miller, D. C., and Form, W. *Industrial sociology.* New York: Harper & Row, 1964 (2nd ed.).
National Vocational Guidance Association. *NVGA bibliography of current occupational literature, 1963 revision.* Washington: Amer. Personnel & Guidance Assoc., 1963.
Quinn, F. X., S.J. (ed.) *The ethical aftermath of automation.* Westminster, Md.: Newman, 1962.
Rosenberg, M. *Occupations and values.* Glencoe, Ill.: Free Press, 1957.
Shartle, C. L. *Occupational information.* Englewood Cliffs, N.J.: Prentice-Hall, 1959 (3rd ed.).
Thorndike, R. L. *Ten thousand careers.* New York: Wiley, 1959.
U.S. Department of Labor. *Occupational outlook handbook.* Washington, 1966.
Warner, W. L. *Occupational mobility.* Minneapolis: Univ. of Minnesota Press, 1955.
Whyte, W. F. et al. *Money and motivation.* New York: Harper, 1955.
Wolfbein, S. L. *Employment and unemployment in the U.S.A.* Chicago: Science Research, 1964.
Zapoleon, Marguerite. *Occupational planning for women.* New York: Harper, 1961.

Anne Anastasi, Ph.D.

is Professor of Psychology, Fordham University Graduate School of Arts and Sciences. She received her bachelor's degree and membership in Phi Beta Kappa at Barnard College and a Ph.D. from Columbia University. She formerly taught at Barnard College, Queens College, University of Wisconsin and University of Minnesota. For several years she was research consultant to the College Entrance Examination Board. At the College Board she has also been Chairman of the Aptitude Testing Committee and the Research and Development Committee. She has held numerous posts in professional psylogical associations, including the presidency of Division 1 of the American Psychological Association. Her major publications are: Differential Psychology, Psychological Testing, *and* Fields of Applied Psychology. *She also collaborated in six other books and has written about 100 monographs and journal articles in the field of psychology.*

Psychology and Guidance

Of the many contributions that psychology can make to guidance, I have chosen four as being of primary importance at the present time. These pertain to: (1) psychological tests; (2) interviewing techniques; (3) the nature of occupational choice; and (4) the counseling process.

PSYCHOLOGICAL TESTS

Psychological tests * may prove helpful in any kind of counseling but they are utilized most often to facilitate educational and vocational decisions. All types of tests may be employed in counseling—and probably are—but certain kinds are more specifically suited to typical counseling needs. *Intelligence tests* are commonly used to determine the individual's general ability level, with special reference to his academic aptitude. It has been repeatedly established that persons engaged in different occupations differ significantly in average intelligence test scores. On the basis of these findings, certain minimum intelligence levels have been identified, below which an individual's chances of success in a particular occupation are slight. There are probably many reasons for these occupational differences, but a major factor is undoubtedly the educational level required for different types of work. The professions and other occupations demanding a high level of educational preparation show a higher average and a narrower range of intelligence test scores than do routine clerical and manual jobs.

Since most intelligence tests are primarily measures of scholastic aptitude, one of their applications to counseling is in predicting educational achievement and in estimating the highest educational level the individual is likely to reach. Intelligence tests are especially useful at the elementary school age, when differentiation into separate abilities has not yet advanced very far. Counselors typically rely on group tests of intelligence, which may of course be administered either individually or in groups, and which are available for different levels ranging from the primary grades to the graduate school.

For educational counseling, intelligence tests are often supplemented with *achievement tests* in different areas. Of particular interest are tests of reading and arithmetic skills. Special disabilities in these skills—particularly in reading—may seriously

* For further information about the tests cited, as well as for other examples, see Anastasi (1961).

25

interfere with overall educational achievement. *Special aptitude tests* are frequently administered in individual cases as demanded by the particular circumstances. When considering a special educational program or when making vocational plans, the counselee may need information about his manual dexterity or other motor skills or about his mechanical, clerical, artistic, or musical aptitudes. Tests are available to aid evaluation in each of these areas.

Multiple aptitude batteries are of particular relevance to counseling problems because they provide a profile of scores in relatively independent abilities. Combining the principal abilities covered by intelligence tests with other broad aptitude areas enables the individual to explore his major strengths and weaknesses. While a global intelligence test score may indicate the general level of expected educational or vocational attainment, a profile of scores on a multiple aptitude battery is more helpful in the choice of a field of specialization.

An example of a well constructed multiple aptitude battery is the Differential Aptitude Tests, commonly known as the DAT. This battery has been in use long enough to permit the accumulation of extensive data on its predictive validity. For this purpose, test scores were checked against performance in many different courses in high schools and colleges, as well as in a variety of jobs. Designed primarily for use in educational and vocational counseling of high school students, this battery yields scores in eight abilities; verbal reasoning, numerical ability, abstract reasoning, space relations, mechanical reasoning, clerical speed and accuracy, spelling, and grammar. Other commercially available batteries have not yet been sufficiently validated to be considered ready for use in individual counseling. * The General Aptitude Test Battery (GATB) developed by the United States Employment Service is also a multiple aptitude battery, but its use is restricted largely to state employment service offices.

Among the most popular counseling instruments are *interest tests*. Basically, these tests are self-report inventories in which

* For a critical evaluation of available multiple aptitude batteries, see Super (1958).

26

the counselee records his likes and dislikes or his relative preferences for many kinds of familiar activities, people, or objects. In the Kuder Preference Record, for example, the individual compares three items in each set, marking the one he likes best and the one he likes least. Thus he may have to indicate whether he would rather visit an art gallery, browse in a library, or visit a museum; or whether he would rather collect autographs, coins, or butterflies. The responses are scored with references to ten broad interest areas: outdoor, mechanical, computational, scientific, persuasive, artistic, literary, musical, social service, and clerical.

A somewhat different approach is illustrated by the Vocational Interest Blank developed by Strong. This test yields separate scores in each of about fifty occupations in the form for men and about thirty in the form for women. Essentially, if a person gets a high score for a given occupation it means that his interests closely resemble those of persons engaged in that occupation. It suggests that he would find that occupation and his colleagues in it congenial and that he would fit well into their way of life. For guidance purposes, the total pattern of occupational scores is customarily taken into account. It may be just as important to know which occupational groups the individual is most unlike as it is to know which groups he resembles most closely.

Other types of *personality tests* are used to a much more limited extent in counseling. The lack of adequate validity data about most of these instruments requires that they be interpreted with considerable caution and checked against other sources of information about the counselee. Personality inventories may be employed as a preliminary screening device to identify persons who should be referred for psychotherapy. Or they may be used by the counselor to focus discussion upon personal problems and to help the counselee to understand his own behavior.

Although originally developed in a clinical setting, the Minnesota Multiphasic Personality Inventory (MMPI) has been used widely in counseling normal persons. A vast amount of research has been conducted with this test, with both normal and pathological samples. On the basis of data obtained from over four thousand cases examined in a college counseling center, a code-book has been prepared for interpreting the MMPI profiles of college students. A few self-report inventories have been specially developed for normal persons and their scores are expressed in terms of needs, motives, and interpersonal response modes rather than in terms of pathological symptoms. Examples of such inventories include the Edwards Personal Preference Schedule, the California Psychological Inventory, and the Minnesota Counseling Inventory. Although these tests are easy to administer and score, they should be used only by a fully trained counseling psychologist. Their scores cannot be taken at face value. They need to be interpreted in terms of available research findings about each test as well as background data about the individual. For information about the counselee's attitudes, motives, social traits, and emotional problems, the counselor should rely chiefly on interviewing techniques and case history material.

INTERVIEWING TECHNIQUES

Psychologists have done much to develop and refine the interview as a data-gathering procedure, especially for use in personnel selection, clinical practice, and counseling (see Bingham *et al.*, 1959; Fear, 1958; Kahn and Cannell, 1957; Maier, 1958). Through face-to-face conversation with the counselee, the interview can provide two major kinds of information, namely, a behavior sample and a reactional biography. As a behavior sample, the interview permits direct observation of certain traits, such as voice, speech, language usage, nervous mannerisms, and general appearance. Since the interview is a dynamic interaction between two persons, it may also yield clues to certain complex social traits, such as poise, tact, aggressiveness, and emotional control.

The second source of interview information is the biographical data reported by the counselee in response to questioning. Such questions should cover not only what has happened to the individual in the past, but also how he reacted to it and how he

28

perceives it—hence, the name reactional biography is applied to this type of data. We want to find out not only what grades he received in school, but also which courses he liked and which he disliked, and why. If an individual was fired from a job following an argument with his boss, does he perceive this incident as an indication of his inadequate self-control, as plain tough luck, or as systematic persecution? The implications would obviously be quite different in the three cases. When properly interpreted, life-history data provide a particularly sound basis for understanding an individual and predicting his future behavior. The life history has been aptly described as "an unbiased population of events which is as convincing an operational definition of a person as one can hope for" (Dailey, 1960, p. 21).

The chief potential contributions of the interview to individual appraisal are threefold. First, it permits the assessment of traits for which no satisfactory tests are as yet available. It would be foolish to try to evaluate an individual's intelligence or mechanical aptitude, for example, through an interview, since tests can do the job quicker and more accurately. For many social, emotional, and motivational traits, however, an intensive interview by a skilled interviewer provides the best source of information.

A second advantage of the interview is that it permits fuller coverage of biographical data than can be achieved through any other procedure available to the counselor. Through selective probing, the interviewer can explore a particular area more intensively as the individual's own remarks point the way. Thus in his search for facts, the interviewer can be guided by the counselee's prior responses. The latter suggest hypotheses that in turn determine the direction of further probing. In this individual adaptability of procedure lies one of the principal advantages of the interview over tests, questionnaires, and other standardized instruments.

A third contribution of the interview is to be found in the opportunities it provides for obtaining a composite picture of the individual. Ideally, the interviewer should integrate facts elicited in the interview with test scores and information gathered from other sources. Such a procedure permits the qualitative interpretation of trait patterns and of the interaction of different factors within the individual. Thus the interpretation of any single fact, such as a test score, can be made contingent upon other facts, such as another test score or some event in the individual's earlier experience. In his interpretation, the interviewer can also incorporate rare events, whose occurrence is too infrequent to permit their use in statistical predictions. Although any one such event rarely occurs, it may significantly affect outcome in an individual case. Breaking one's right arm just before final examinations in one's junior year at college may be a rare event, but it is important for the student to whom it happens—and it may mark a turning point in his life, for better or for worse. Moreover, *different* "rare events" will be encountered often enough to have a substantial effect upon the decisions reached in large numbers of cases. In this connection, we may recall the old paradox that "an improbable event is one that hardly ever happens, but nevertheless something improbable happens almost every day."

With regard to the interviewing process itself, psychologists have worked out certain guidelines. For fact-finding purposes, the most effective type of interview is the patterned interview. In it, the interviewer undertakes to cover certain specified areas, such as education, work history, early home background, present familial situation, and recreational activities. Each of these areas is introduced by asking a comprehensive standardized question. Within these limits, however, the interviewer has considerable latitude. His role is to steer the conversation into relevant channels and make sure that all areas are adequately explored. Through follow-up questions, he checks on any points that have been omitted or glossed over by the client. He thus serves as a master of ceremonies who runs the show but lets the client perform.

The nondirective or client-centered interview is much more unstructured than the patterned interview. The client-centered interview provides maximum freedom for the client to bring up topics for discussion and to pursue them in his own fashion. This type of interview is more likely to be employed in counseling for emotional problems, but it may be used for all counseling purposes. The choice of interviewing technique depends chiefly on the theoretical orientation and training of the particular counselor.

Whichever interviewing technique is employed, a major requirement is the establishment of good rapport between interviewer and client. Essentially this means that the client must have confidence in the interviewer, so that he feels free to communicate. Most people show some resistance to talking about themselves. When the matters under consideration are emotionally charged, the resistance may even extend to thinking about them. There are several ways in which the counselor can help to overcome this resistance. Privacy and confidentiality are of course basic to the counseling relationship. The client must feel sure that nothing he tells the counselor will be repeated to any other person. Through his own remarks and behavior, moreover, the counselor can show that he is interested, attentive, and seriously concerned about the client's problems. The counselor's manner should be warm, friendly, and relaxed, while remaining impersonal and professional.

Most counseling psychologists today try to establish a permissive atmosphere in the counseling situation. By this is meant that the counselor refrains from judging or evaluating anything the client communicates. He expresses neither approval nor disapproval but concentrates on understanding and clarifying the client's own feelings. Although permissiveness is most closely identified with client-centered counseling, its advantages—at least at certain stages of counseling—are recognized by most counseling psychologists, regardless of their theoretical persuasion.

Effective interviewing requires skill in data gathering and data interpreting. An interview may lead to wrong decisions because important facts were not elicited or because the available facts were inadequately or incorrectly interpreted. A major qualification of the successful interviewer is sensitivity in picking up clues in the subject's behavior or in the facts he reports. Such clues provide the interviewer with hypotheses. They should lead to further probing for additional facts that may either verify or contradict each hypothesis.

A good interviewer needs much more than an interest in people and a pleasant manner. Interviewing skills can be developed and improved through training. Among the methods employed for such training are direct observation of interviews conducted by skilled interviewers, listening to tape recordings, reading transcripts of interviews, role playing in which trainees assume in turn the roles of interviewer and interviewee, and supervised practice in interviewing genuine clients. Discussion of the content of these interviews with other trainees and with an instructor is most fruitful. Even listening to a tape recording of one's own interview without benefit of comments by others can be highly instructive! This practical training should be accompanied by an introduction to interviewing principles and a consideration of common hazards to be avoided.

The psychological literature provides a good deal of information about possible pitfalls in interviewing (see Anastasi, 1964, Ch. 4). There is, for example, the halo effect. This refers to the fact that a single trait in which an individual is conspicuously superior or inferior may cast a "halo" over his other traits and thus raise or lower his ratings in all traits. If a person has an alert and attentive manner, for instance, he may be judged intelligent, cooperative, and dependable, even when he is quite deficient in all these qualities. Or a superb craftsman capable of turning out extremely precise work may give an impression of sloppy workmanship because he is carelessly dressed.

Judgment errors may also arise from social stereotypes. Controlled experiments have demonstrated, for example, that ratings for such traits as intelligence, industriousness, talkativeness, and conscientiousness may be influenced by the wearing of spectacles or the use of lipstick. Other stereotypes stemming from folklore or from the pseudosciences of phrenology and physiognomy may also affect ratings in many psychological traits. The association of a high forehead with intelligence, a square jaw with determination, or a steady look with honesty are familiar examples. Such stereotypes may affect ratings even when the rater is unaware of their operation. What the interviewer accepts as a hunch or an intuition may in fact stem from an unrecognized response to an irrelevant physical clue.

Some hunches arise from a chance resemblance to someone the interviewer may have known in the past. Suppose a former acquaintance who proved to be irresponsible happened to have eyes that were spaced far apart. When the interviewer encounters someone else with the same facial anomaly, he may respond with a vague feeling of distrust. Not being able to identify the source of his distrust, he is likely to attribute it to an intuition or a hunch and accept it without further ado. When we recognize that hunches are in fact immediate responses to minor cues, we can see that they should be neither accepted nor summarily rejected; they should be scrutinized. First, we should try to discover the basis of the hunch. Identifying the initiating cue will in itself go far toward showing whether the hunch was based on a stereotype or chance resemblance, or whether it occurred in response to a relevant fact in the individual's behavior. Second, we should regard the hunch not as conclusive in itself but as a hypothesis to be tested by further probing.

As a final example, we may consider contagious bias. This error refers to the effect that the interviewer's own beliefs, expectations, or preconceived notions may have upon the client's responses. The interviewer may inadvertently inject his ideas into the conversation by the way he frames his questions, by selectively reinforcing certain types of answers, or by misunderstanding ambiguous responses. He may also slant results by following up some cues while ignoring others. This selective probing has been described as "soliciting" to distinguish it from unbiased probing. It is a means of seeking out data to support a preconceived notion, rather than to test a hypothesis that may be accepted or rejected. Contagious bias is one of the most difficult pitfalls to avoid in interviewing. There is evidence that, even in nondirective counseling by highly trained counselors, the client's responses are affected by subtle and unintentional expressions of approval or disapproval on the part of the counselor (see Anastasi, 1964, pp. 402-403).

THE NATURE OF OCCUPATIONAL CHOICE

The most distinctive area of research in counseling psychology is that dealing with occupational choices. What factors determine such choices? When and under what circumstances are vocational decisions made? What kinds of satisfactions do individuals seek in their work? How do these satisfactions differ among persons who choose different occupations? That counseling psychologists should focus upon occupations in their research programs is understandable for a number of reasons. First there is the historical association of counseling with vocational problems. Modern counseling psychology originated in the vocational guidance movement. Even today, when the scope of counseling has broadened considerably, many counseling psychologists still function predominantly in the vocational area.

Even more important is the increasing realization that occupation itself plays a central role in one's total life adjustment. Emotional problems often arise from job tensions and frustrations, while absorbing and rewarding work can be highly therapeutic. Similarly, maladjustments can frequently be prevented by engaging in satisfying work activities. Not only the work itself, but also its many associated experiences, can contribute to the individual's total adjustment. Of considerable importance to mental health, for instance, are acceptance by fellow workers and the feelings of security and belongingness that come from identification with an occupational group.

In a very real sense, choosing an occupation is equivalent to choosing a way of life. For one thing, the individual spends a large proportion of his waking time on the job. But the influence of one's occupation extends well beyond working hours. For the large majority of people in our culture, the nature of their work is the single most important determiner of social status. When trying to "place" a new acquaintance, people ask, "What *is* Jones?" and are told that he is a lawyer, or an insurance salesman, or a plumber. The income derived from work helps to shape one's general style of living—the neighborhood in which he resides, the sort of house or apartment he occupies, the car he drives, the kind of vacation he can afford.

Occupations differ in many other ways that may be significant to the individual worker. They may determine one's work and leisure schedule, the part of the country where he must live, and his habitual dress—as illustrated by our stereotypes of white-collar and blue-collar jobs and of the business man in the grey flannel suit. Friendships are often work-determined. People tend to spend their leisure hours with co-workers, business associates, or professional colleagues. Nor is it at all unusual for an individual to marry someone he or she has met through job contacts.

Many kinds of work are associated with characteristic sets of values that frequently extend into one's personal life. If some of these values are not consonant with the individual's own values, the resulting conflict may be quite disruptive. From a different angle, the choice of an occupation can be described as a way of establishing one's identity. Donald Super, who has written extensively on this subject, points out that vocational choice is the implementation of a self concept. He maintains that "satisfaction in one's work and on one's job depends on the extent to which the work, the job, and the way of life that goes with them, enable one to play the kind of role that one wants to play" (Super, 1953, p. 189).

More specifically, occupations are chosen to meet needs. The economic need to earn one's livelihood is only one of many such needs. It can usually be met by any one of many jobs, among which the individual must choose on the basis of other needs. For one person, for example, the need for personal freedom and independence may be so strong that he can only be happy as a free-lance or self-employed worker. Another may function best when he is the center of attention—a need that could be satisfied by many occupations, ranging from actor to information clerk. Still another may require the security that comes from working in a highly structured situation in which he is relieved of all responsibility for decision-making.

These needs are not necessarily verbalized. The individual may simply feel that he *must* paint or that an office job is not for him, without being able to explain why. It is one of the objectives of counseling to make the individual aware of the motives underlying such convictions. When needs are recognized as such, they are more readily brought under rational control and are less likely to lead to unrealistic decisions. Throughout this process, however, the counselor must operate within the framework of the *client's* needs and values, which may differ from those of the counselor. This is one of the reasons why the counselor cannot choose a "suitable" occupation for the client without at least some interaction with the client.

One of the most important objectives of all counseling is to facilitate the making of effective decisions. In contrast to the charlatan, who is likely to hand his client a ready-made solution for his problems or to choose a specific occupation for him, the professional counselor concentrates on improving the individual's own decision-making. Effective vocational decisions require accurate knowledge regarding both abilities and wants or needs. Tests help in this connection, as does much of the verbal interaction betweeen counselor and counselee. In addition, effective vocational decisions require knowledge about occupations, which counseling likewise endeavors to provide. Finally, they require the ability to think clearly—the ability to combine available information in predicting outcomes, to weigh alternative courses of action, and to make choices that adequately reflect all relevant factors.

Vocational planning normally involves, not one decision, but a multitude of decisions extending over a period of many years. A long series of preliminary decisions regarding courses of study, training programs, and trial jobs may have to be made and implemented before the individual finally enters his chosen field of work. Moreover, people's wants and their suitability for different careers may change over time. Jobs also change. In our rapidly evolving society, new fields of work constantly emerge, and even familiar jobs may become drastically altered. All these circumstances call for flexibility in the vocational decisions made at any one stage. Also relevant is the multipotentiality of both persons and jobs. Any one person is qualified for many different jobs, not just for a single job. Conversely, a given occupation may be successfully pursued in many different ways by different persons. The goal of vocational counseling is *not* early commitment to an ultimate vocational choice. Rather, counseling should contribute toward the improvement of vocational decisions made throughout the life span.

Psychological research on vocational decisions has barely begun, but it is a growing field of investigation. Recent developments in decision theory provide a theoretical framework within which vocational choices can be systematically analyzed. Decision theory began as an attempt to put the decision-making process into mathematical form so that available information may be used to arrive at the most effective decision under given conditions. The mathematical procedures required by decision theory are often quite complex, and few are in a form permitting their immediate application to counseling problems. Neverthless, the basic concepts of decision theory help in formulating and clarifying the decision process (Bross, 1953; Edwards, 1954).

Essentially, decisions require three types of information: 1) the predicted probabilities of different outcomes; 2) estimates of the risks involved or the consequences of failure; and 3) the relative values or importance of different goals. In vocational decisions, data for predicting outcomes include information about the individual's capabilities, derived from tests and other sources, as well as job information. Thus the individual, with the help of the counselor, might estimate his chances of completing an apprenticeship as machinist or of graduating from medical school. The consequences of making a bad decision help to establish the certainty level we require to take action. If the consequences of failure are slight, we may be willing to try a course of action even though there may be a high probability of failure. Both decision theory and counseling recognize the fundamental importance of values in the decision process. To be workable, the individual's decisions must be consonant with his own value system.

The recognition that vocational decisions are made over a period of many years has led to the concept of vocational development. Super (1957) describes five stages of vocational development. The first is the *growth* stage, extending from birth to about the age of fourteen. During this period, the child begins to develop a self concept. Through observation of parents and other adults in the family, he first becomes acquainted with different roles that an individual may play in his culture. As he grows older, his available role models increase through his experiences in school and other situations outside the home. Still other roles may be encountered vicariously in books, movies, or television.

In play and fantasy, the child may begin to "try on" some of these roles at an early age. Later on, he has increasing opportunities for realistic tryouts of vocational roles. As he (or she) performs household chores, works in the yard, baby-sits, tinkers with mechanical gadgets, plays baseball, takes violin lessons, or studies different subjects in school, the process of reality testing begins.

The second stage proposed by Super is that of *exploration,* covering adolescence and early adulthood. This is a period of extensive reality testing, with resulting modification of the self concept. It is at this stage that important educational choices are first faced and vocational goals are first seriously examined. For these reasons, vocational counseling has traditionaly focused on this period. At this stage the individual also undertakes more formal work tryouts through part-time, temporary, and trial jobs.

The third stage is that of *establishment.* After some preliminary trial-and-error and floundering, most persons tend to "settle down" in one line of work. Stabilization and advancement are typical of this stage. The individual comes to identify with his chosen field of work; he accumulates experience, which in turn ties him more closely to that field; and he assimilates the general way of life associated with his job. The fourth stage is one of *maintenance.* Continuing in the same field of work, the individual at middle age typically concentrates on retaining the position he has attained on the job, at home, and in the community. This stage leads finally to occupational *decline,* as indicated by reduction in vocational activities and eventual retirement.

Like any system of stages employed to describe human development, this schema is admittedly an oversimplification. The development process is continuous and any description of it in terms of stages is only an approximation. Moreover, individuals differ widely in the time of onset and duration of each stage. In some persons, one or more stages may be completely absent. When these limitations are recognized, however, these stages can provide a convenient framework for describing vocational problems characteristic of different life periods. And they can help to establish norms against which individual development can be evaluated.

A related concept is that of developmental tasks. In vocational development, as in other aspects of human development, the individual must meet different demands and undertake different developmental tasks at each age from the preschool period to the age of retirement. Vocational maturity can be measured in terms of the individual's mastery of the developmental tasks appropriate to his life stage. Working within this theoretical framework, Super and his associates (Super *et al.*, 1957; Super and Overstreet, 1960) have initiated a twenty-year longitudinal research project with approximately one hundred ninth-grade boys. The object of this study is to identify the vocational developmental tasks appropriate to each age level and to establish developmental norms for each age. At the ninth-grade level, for example, typical indices of vocational maturity include awareness of the need for making vocational choices and knowledge of factors affecting choice, acceptance of responsibility for choice and planning, and use of resources in obtaining occupational information. Thus for the ninth-grade boy, vocational maturity is defined, not by the wisdom or consistency of the ultimate vocational goal he chooses, but rather by the way he handles the preliminary planning and exploration required at this stage.

THE COUNSELING PROCESS

As you are well aware, there are many varieties of counseling. Besides vocational counseling, those in which psychologists have been most closely involved include educational counseling in schools and colleges, employee counseling in industry, rehabilitation counseling of the physically handicapped, old-age counseling, and marriage counseling. Personal counseling with regard to emotional problems runs through all other forms of counseling. Many clients seek the help of a counselor explicitly because of an emotional problem. But even when the referral problem concerns a vocational decision, an educational question, or some other specific and relatively "impersonal" matter, the root of the difficulty often lies in a personality problem. Inability to arrive at a satisfactory vocational decision, for example, may itself result from emotional immaturity, insecurity, unwillingness to face reality, or a difficult interpersonal relation within the family. Moreover, personality difficulties frequently complicate and aggravate other problems.

It is in the area of personal counseling that the psychologist can make his most distinctive contribution. Furthermore, the counseling psychologist recognizes the close interrelation of all adjustment problems and therefore functions at a broad level regardless of the type of counseling involved. His orientation tends always to be toward counseling the whole person.

When viewed thus broadly, the counseling process includes much more than fact-finding and information-giving. What else does the counselor do? What techniques are available to him to help the client work through his anxieties, hostilities, and insecurities so that he can think rationally about his problems and reach wise decisions? What, in brief, are the distinctive features of the counseling process?

First, counseling consists in a verbal interaction between two persons. To put it simply, the client talks about his problems with the counselor. The client is encouraged to verbalize his feelings and examine his problems fully. Through such self-exploration, the individual gains a better understanding of his own motives and actions. This insight, it is believed, will help him bring his feelings under rational control and deal more effectively with his problems. The attainment of insight by the client is a major goal of most forms of counseling.

Counseling also involves learning. The individual acquired his maladaptive responses through past learning. One of the objects of counseling is to enable him to unlearn these responses and replace them with new responses of a more adaptive nature. Providing practice in decision-making is another way in which the learning process enters into counseling. In his interactions with the counselor, the individual gradually discovers that, no matter what he says, he will not be criticized, blamed, or rejected. The strict confidentiality observed also reassures him that his behavior during the counseling hour will lead to no aversive consequences in his daily life. Counseling thus provides a "safe" situation in which the individual can try out new interpersonal behavior. The learner can make mistakes without danger. The client's interaction with the counselor helps him to understand his reactions to people in general and enables him to develop new ways of feeling and thinking about himself and others.

In the opinion of most counseling psychologists, the heart of the counseling process is the interpersonal relationship between counselor and client. In this respect, counseling psychology reflects most clearly the influence of the nondirective or client-centered school of Carl Rogers (1942, 1951, 1961). The basic postulate of client-centered counseling is that the individual has the capacity to identify the sources of his emotional problems and to work out effective solutions, once he is freed from disabling anxieties and feelings of insecurity. To accomplish this goal, the client-centered counselor establishes a permissive, accepting, and non-threatening relationship. He refrains from probing, interpreting, advising, persuading, or suggesting. He serves the function of active listener, trying to understand fully what the client says and feels, and making every effort to perceive situations from the client's point of view. An important part of the counselor's task is to reflect and clarify the client's feelings by restating the client's remarks. It is in this way that the counselor plays the part of *active* listener. And it is this reflection of feeling that requires the greatest understanding and skill on the part of the counselor.

41

In keeping with the emphasis upon the counseling process itself as a means of contributing to the client's development, counseling psychologists have given considerable attention to the way tests are introduced into this process (Bordin, 1955; Goldman, 1961; Tyler, 1961). Some feel that what tests are chosen and how the client scores on them are less important questions than how the tests are incorporated into the counseling process. Taking tests is itself a significant experience for the client. It is a kind of "reality testing," providing the client with an opportunity to check his aspirations, plans, and self concept against objective standards. Unlike test scores obtained in other situations, the information obtained from counseling tests is primarily for the use of the client himself, to help him in reaching decisions.

In nondirective counseling, the client frequently participates in the selection of tests. Some counselors introduce no tests at all unless or until the client requests them. Others regularly employ tests, but ask the client to choose those he would like to take from a given list. Client participation in test selection has many advantages over a completely counselor-directed program. If the client cannot see the relevance of the tests to his immediate problem, he may simply drop out of counseling The same result may follow if the client is not emotionally ready to submit to a realistic appraisal of himself. When he is convinced of the need for testing and understands its purpose, on the other hand, he will be better motivated to do his best on ability tests and to answer frankly on self-report inventories. He will also be more likely to accept test findings, rather than reacting defensively toward them.

One final point should be noted regarding the nature of the counseling process. In contrast to psychotherapy, counseling seeks to utilize the individual's psychological resources rather than trying to change his basic personality structure. For example, if a client has deep-rooted feelings of insecurity, the psychotherapist typically attempts to alter the client's personality so that he may overcome his insecurity, whereas the counselor may help the client choose a vocation in which emotional insecurity is not a

42

serious drawback. Counseling focuses on positive strengths to be developed, rather than on defects to be eliminated. The counselor is not concerned so much with ferreting out personality deficiencies that may already be under adequate control. Rather he concentrates on assets that can be mobilized. The counselor looks for the normalities found even in abnormal persons, whereas the clinical psychologist—and, to a greater extent, the psychiatrist—looks for the abnormalities found even in normal persons. In its emphasis upon positive development and the prevention of maladjustment, counseling is consistent with the aims of the current mental health movement (Joint Commission for Mental Illness and Health, 1961). Perhaps as we learn more about the causes and prevention of mental disorders, there will be an increasing utilization of counselors and a decreasing need for therapists.

REFERENCES

Anastasi, Anne. *Psychological testing* (2nd ed.). New York: Macmillan, 1961.

Anastasi, Anne. *Fields of applied psychology.* New York: McGraw-Hill, 1964.

Bingham, W. V., Moore, B. V., and Gustad, J. W. *How to interview* (4th ed.). New York: Harper & Row, 1959.

Bordin, E. S. *Psychological counseling.* New York: Appleton-Century-Crofts, 1955.

Bross, I. D. J. *Design for decision.* New York: Macmillan, 1953.

Dailey, C. A. The life history as a criterion of assessment. *J. counsel. Psychol.,* 1960, *7,* 20-23.

Edwards, W. The theory of decision making. *Psychol. Bull.,* 1954, *51,* 380-417.

Fear, R. A. *The evaluation interview: Predicting job performance in business and industry.* New York: McGraw-Hill, 1958.

Goldman, L. *Using tests in counseling.* New York: Appleton-Century-Crofts, 1961.

Joint Commission on Mental Illness and Health. *Action for mental health: Final report of the Joint Commission on Mental Illness and Health.* New York: Basic Books, 1961.

Kahn, R. L., and Cannel, C. F. *The dynamics of interviewing: Theory, technique, and cases.* New York: Wiley, 1957.

Maier, N. R. F. *The appraisal interview: Objectives, methods, and skills.* New York: Wiley, 1958.

Rogers, C. R. *Counseling and psychotherapy: Newer concepts in practice.* Boston: Houghton Mifflin, 1942.

Rogers, C. R. *Client-centered therapy: Its current practice, implications, and theory.* Boston: Houghton Mifflin, 1951.

Rogers, C. R. *On becoming a person: A therapist's view of psychotherapy.* Boston: Houghton Mifflin, 1961.

Super, D. E. A theory of vocational development. *Amer. Psychologist,* 1953, 8, 185-190.

Super, D. E. *The psychology of careers; an introduction to vocational development.* New York: Harper & Row, 1957.

Super, D. E. (Ed.). The use of multifactor tests in guidance. Washington: Amer. Personnel Guid. Assoc., 1958. (Repr. from *Personnel Guid. J.,* 1956-1957.)

Super, D. E., *et al. Vocational development: A framework for research.* New York: Teach. Coll., Columbia Univer., Bur. Publ., 1957.

Super, D. E., and Overstreet, Phoebe L. *The vocational maturity of ninth grade boys.* New York Teach. Coll., Columbia Univer., Bur. Publ., 1960.

Tyler, Leona E. *The work of the counselor* (2nd ed.). New York: Appleton-Century-Crofts, 1961.

ADDITIONAL READING

Adams, J. F. *Problems in counseling, a case study approach.* New York: Macmillan, 1962.

Allport, G. W. *Pattern and growth in personality.* New York: Holt, Rinehart & Winston, 1961.

Bier, W. C., S.J. (ed.). *The adolescent: his search for understanding.* New York: Fordham University Press, 1963.

Buchheimer, A., and Balogh, Sara C. *The counseling relationship, a casebook.* Chicago: Science Research Associates, 1961.

Byrne, R. H. *The school counselor.* Boston: Houghton Mifflin, 1963.

Cronbach, L. J. *Educational psychology.* New York: Harcourt, Brace & World, 1963 (2nd ed.).

Erickson, C. E. *The counseling interview.* New York: Prentice-Hall, 1960.

Hahn, M. E., and MacLean, M. S. *Counseling psychology.* New York: McGraw-Hill, 1955 (2nd ed.).

McGowan, J. F., and Schmidt, L. D. *Counseling: readings in theory and practice.* New York: Holt, Rinehart & Winston, 1962.

Schneiders, A. *Personality development and adjustment in adolescence.* Milwaukee: Bruce, 1960.

Sechrest, Carolyn. *New dimensions in counseling students, a case approach.* New York: Bureau of Publications, Teachers College, Columbia University, 1958.

Shaffer, L. F., and Shoben, E. J. *The psychology of adjustment: a dynamic and experimental approach to mental hygiene.* Boston: Houghton Mifflin, 1956 (2nd ed.).

Stagner, R. *Psychology of personality.* New York: McGraw-Hill, 1961 (3rd ed.).

Steimel, R. J. (ed.). *Psychological counseling of adolescents.* Washington, D.C.: Catholic University of America Press, 1962.

Symonds, P. M. *What education has to learn from psychology.* New York: Bureau of Publications, Teachers College, Columbia U., 1958.

Thorpe, L. P. *Psychological foundations of personality.* New York: McGraw-Hill, 1938.

Woodworth, R. S. *The dynamics of behavior.* New York: Holt, Rinehart & Winston, 1958.

Valett, R. E. *The practice of school psychology: professional problems.* New York: Wiley, 1963.

Francis C. Bauer, M.D.

*is the director of the Student Adjustment
Center which provides psychiatric, psychological and social casework service to fifteen
school districts in Suffolk County, New York.
He serves the dioceses of Brooklyn and Rock-
ville Centre in the capacity of psychiatric
consultant and is a professorial lecturer in
psychology at St. John's University. He received his B.S. degree at St. John's University and an M.D. at the Georgetown Medical
School and did graduate work in psychiatry
at Pilgrim State Hospital and the New
York State Psychiatric Institute. Dr. Bauer
has been the Director of the Manhattan
After-Care Clinic in New York City and the
Child Guidance Clinic in Bay Shore, Long
Island. He was a delegate to the 1960 White
House Conference on Children and Youth
and is currently a member of the Governor's
Committee concerned with the follow-up of
the White House Conference. Recent ar-
ticles in the* New York Times *by Dr. Bauer
include:* "The Junior Rat Race," "The
Plight of the Brand New Parent," *and*
"Mothers Shouldn't Smother."

Guidance and Psychiatry

Very recently I had an opportunity to learn something about
guidance programs in the schools from the standpoint of administration. The occasion was a meeting of secondary school
principals representing fifteen districts in a suburban area with
a total school population of about 85,000 children. What I
learned was both interesting and revealing. It was new to me

46

but may be something which guidance people have suspected for a long time. I learned that few educators know what guidance really is and even fewer know what guidance ought to be.

The administrators in this instance demonstrated the same inconsistencies as those common to most textbooks on the subject. They were unable, for example, to make the descriptions of their own programs conform to any acceptable definition of guidance. They were unable to make the distinction between the guidance process and counseling, one of its techniques. They could not clearly define the role of the guidance counselor but were of a consensus that the training institutions were doing a decidedly inferior job in turning out competent people. And, as do all of the textbooks, the principals agreed that guidance is for everybody in the school system. Having done this, however, they, again like the books, proceeded to discuss guidance only in terms of problem children, emotional disturbances, and socioeconomic disadvantage. It was, at the risk of sounding critical, a typically successful meeting in which the administrators concluded that they had people on their staffs of whom they did not know quite what to ask and who, in any event, were not properly trained to do a job, the nature of which they themselves had failed to define.

Lest the guidance people in the group feel too comfortable with what appears thus far to be an assault on administration, let me assure you that the case could be stated, and with equal facility, in such a manner that guidance rather than administration would be the victim. Perhaps, at this point, before you yield to the temptation to categorize me as a chronic objector, I had best move on to the stated purpose of this paper.

THE IMPACT OF FREUD

When the early followers of Sigmund Freud brought his message to the world, they did so with a lack of becoming modesty and in a very short period of time, the principles of dynamic psychiatry began to exert considerable influence on every aspect of living. Because these principles dealt with the individual and embraced concepts of personal worth and fulfillment, the impact of the new science was felt primarily by the Western world. Perhaps, too, because the problems of the universe were known to be clearly solvable in time, there was a tendency for man to focus attention on himself and to indulge his proclivity to introspection. Having discovered a previously unknown area of mental activity in the unconscious, and being assured that such activity influences to a greater or lesser degree what appeared to be entirely voluntary behavior, it is not surprising that concepts of law, ethics, politics and religion were soon the subjects of re-examination.

Guidance services were already a part of many school systems at the time of the psychiatric revolution. Although the emphasis then was entirely vocational, the services nevertheless provided a fertile field for the injection of psychological and psychoanalytic ideas. There followed an expansion of the concept of guidance to include various notions of democracy and equality, a broader and improved educational program, attention to moral and religious values and, finally, to socioeconomic conditions. Ultimately, guidance recognized the presence of inner needs and attempted to utilize these in motivation. It is in this area that psychiatry has made its greatest contribution to the guidance field.

The search for causes of pathological anxiety and other neurotic symptoms was completely unrewarding as long as man was thought of biologically as a purely somatic entity endowed with intelligence. All aberrant behavior, every deviation from some expected norm and an inability to adjust to life and its vicissitudes had, in this system, to be attributed to some organic disorder or structural change which should be grossly or microscopically demonstrable. It was not until man's inner psychic life was explored that we began to see the human organism as a dynamic entity, a psychosomatic unit of even greater complexity than the biologists had supposed, comprising many parts each of which was in delicate balance with another. It took an even longer period of time spent both in research and speculation to realize that in addition to the internal balances, man had also to react to his environment and maintain some equilibrium with external forces. It is now widely accepted that since there is often conflict between man's inner needs or desires on the one hand and the often harsh demands of reality on the other, the life process is in effect the achievement of a series of equilibria. Each time that significant change occurs within the being as the result of ill health, severe trauma, or other cause, and each time there is a major change in the external environment, it becomes necessary to reach a new equilibrium. It should be emphasized that in most situations the reactions fortunately are automatic and, in many instances, they occur quite apart from any conscious awareness of the fact that adjustments are taking place at all.

THE PRINCIPLE OF EQUILIBRIUM

The application of this principle to guidance is of course elementary. The youngster who is blissfully unaware that he is eminently unqualified for a specific endeavor is deftly made aware by the competent counselor of other areas of activity for which he shows greater aptitude. The counselor is aiding the mechanisms of compensation or substitution to avoid conflict and the outcome is usually satisfactory.

The misapplication of this principle, however, can sometimes be disastrous. This frequently occurs when we fail to recognize that people sometimes function more efficiently when a state of moderate disequilibrium exists. If we are aware of the inner forces in operation and we recognize the demands of reality or the limitations of environment, we sense an almost irresistible impulse to tamper with one or to manipulate the other in order to guarantee adjustment. I should like, however, to challenge the assumption that maximum adjustment is always desirable. It is altogether possible that the emphasis on emotional well-being, feelings of adequacy, security and belonging, while advantageous to the individual in one sense, may subordinate social need and attention to obligation and duty.

I would like to be facetious in order to make the point more clearly. If Nathan Hale had correctly evaluated the situation and had had his basic hostilities removed by analysis, he may very well have been too well adjusted to risk hanging. If Paul Revere had reached a more satisfactory equilibrium, he may well have decided that he was not the only man in Boston with a horse. If Columbus had been too well adjusted to argue with royalty, English might not be our mother tongue. If Michelangelo, Gauguin, and Van Gogh had sustained no childhood trauma and had received in full measure the love and affection and sense of belonging which is now deemed so necessary, they would not have had to sublimate their unconscious drives into the world's greatest art. And if Thomas Edison had been placed in a special class for physically handicapped and discouraged because of deafness from experimenting with, of all things, sound, our world would be quite different today. What I am saying, simply, is that in incorporating principles of psychiatry, guidance must be cautioned to avoid the dangers of excess and of taking too literally the things psychiatrists seem to be saying.

THE INTERVIEW

Guidance, like psychiatry, is a verbal specialty and, as such, involves the interview. The interview is communication between two people, one of whom is usually assumed to be in control by virtue of his knowing what is going on. It should be noted that this assumption could also in some instances be challenged. In any event, the interview, as a device, can be used at any of three levels.

The collection of data, so essential to any evaluative process, is the most superficial use and here especially the interview has become a widely accepted technique for which there is, in my opinion, no substitute. Numerous questionnaires have been designed in the interest of saving time and allegedly of preserving objectivity; but if you want to know what a person is really like, you will have to talk to him sooner or later. The data, for example, obtained from the five hundred and sixty-six questions on the Minnesota Multiphasic Personality Inventory enables one to reach conclusions and to construct a profile with a high degree of accuracy. The same questions, however, put to the person in a structured interview yields data of a more comprehensive and ultimately more useful type. Guidance has learned from psychiatry that what a person says is less important than the way in which he says it. The non-verbal communication transmitted by affect or emotional tone, by accompanying gestures and facial expressions, by the degree of psychomotor activity, by muscular contractions and vasomotor responses is usually of far more significance than the content itself.

The uncovering process of the interview can be used at a deeper level and it is in this area that some counselors have difficulty. To reach deeply into the unconscious and to expose those exquisitely sensitive areas around which defenses have been so carefully constructed is, in my judgment, the exclusive task of the experienced therapist. As such, it appears to me, to be outside the training of the school counselor and beyond the purview of guidance.

I would quarrel with Professors Hatch and Stefflre [1] who state:

The process of adjustment may be thought of as having two major parts: (1) insight, and (2) the manipulation of environment. The first goal in helping an individual to improve his adjustment is to assist him in an objective self-analysis. . . .
Maximum adjustment is possible when the individual has an objective understanding of self, an emotional acceptance of all factors and the environment can be altered to meet his needs.

Obviously, the professor has succumbed to the temptation I mentioned earlier. What I am really quarreling about, I suppose, is that he uses terms like "insight" and "objective self-analysis" and makes it all sound so easy. I doubt very much that the average guidance counselor is aware of the transference reactions which accompany the process of analysis and the gaining of insight. I have even graver doubts about his capacity to handle transference when it is recognized. Again, a matter of consideration is that only the experienced psychotherapist fully appreciates the fact that insight can sometimes be dangerous and a goal in therapy may be to prevent certain insights from ever becoming apparent!

To give only one example of this, let me cite the well documented psychiatric principle that paranoid trends in surface behavior have their roots in deeply unconscious homosexual fears. It is not necessary, I assure you, to prove this point repeatedly at the expense of a succession of patients. It is the exceptional patient who can be brought to that depth of insight since the majority would become more disturbed in the process.

The interview as a counseling technique is indispensable but here, too, the question of training must be considered. I say this because counseling seems to have become a separate subspecialty quite distinct from guidance. At least this is what I infer from reading Professor Arbuckle of Boston University.[2] In his description of the counseling process he says:

A girl may be disturbed about her sexual relations with a boy [I presume we are not dealing here with guidance in the elementary school] because of lack of information and a sex habits inventory would give the counselor some indication of her sex knowledge. He may then present her with some of the information she lacks but this again is not counseling, although it might be guidance.

If, then, there is this distinction between guidance and counseling and the latter has become so highly specialized, I would suggest that the distinction be preserved and that, in order to avoid confusion, the use of the title guidance counselor be discontinued, since it appears to be a contradiction in terms. I would also suggest that the training of the counselor include a great deal more supervised experience in psychological and psychiatric practice than is currently offered.

PSYCHOLOGICAL TESTING

The extent to which inventories, intelligence tests, and projective batteries are used in the guidance process is, I suppose, as variable as the use to which the counselor puts the material thus elicited. Generally speaking, testing is certainly necessary but the amount of testing and the weight assigned in the total evaluation are certainly valid subjects of debate. Here again, we find it unfortunate that professional contests are waged in the arena of the school and often at the expense of the child. Intelligence tests, achievement tests, and projective tests are essential to a total evaluation, especially in children whose problems are not usually sufficiently crystallized to be totally accessible at interview. But any test is a part of the process and must never be permitted to substitute for the whole. They must be used with discretion and the results should be confirmed through other types of observation and examination. Once more the admonition of psychiatry would be to take nothing at its face value and to avoid extremism. No testing at all, as has recently been suggested in some areas, is as absurd a policy as a complete projective battery on every child regardless of clinical indications.

I cannot, at this point, resist quoting from the essay of an unknown author who had just been placed in a class for retarded children. The youngster commented on the test used and made reference to his low I.Q. Among other comments, he said: [3]

Look at this (test). It was so funny I tore out the page and kept it. See three pictures—a tree—a fish—and a cake of ice. I'll read what it tells you to do. 'John is ten years old and his sister is eight. If John is not Mary's brother, draw a line from the fish to the cake of ice. If Mary and John are twins, write your middle name under the tree and if you have no middle name, put a zero there. If they are not twins, print your last name on the tree. If Mary is younger than John, write the Roman number eight in the upper left hand corner of the page; but if John is older than Mary, draw a cat in the lower right hand corner. If they both go to school, write your full name at the bottom of the paper.' I'm never sure how to spell my name so I didn't even try this one.

Psychological tests, especially the projective variety, were designed to bypass conscious awareness and bring forth purely unconscious material. There is an unfortunate tendency, however, to lose sight of this fact and to treat the test responses as if they were consciously motivated and enjoyed the sanction of the super-ego. When this is done, the scores are often applied with mathematical precision to a table of interpretations, certain combinations of which add up to diagnostic entities. In many instances, not enough, if any, attention is paid to the system of defenses built up by the individual against the unconscious trends revealed by the test. Guidance and counseling, it seems to me, would be better kept at the conscious level of functioning in an attempt to strengthen the ego defenses rather than to become involved in the unconscious processes.

CONSULTANTS

In this connection the efficient guidance program should allow for the liberal use of consultants. And the department should know how to use consultation services properly. The counselor, the psychologist, psychiatrist, and social worker have need of each other's services and should not attempt to substitute one for the other. Neither should any of them be threatened by the different professional competence of any other. All too often this team approach about which we hear so much is really perceived by its members as a kind of hierarchy in which one member is liable to dominate the others. But this should not be so. In the consultation process, neither the client nor the consultant should be thrown to the wolves. As a consultant to a number of large school systems offering a combination of kindergarten through doctoral programs, I have had experience of both types. I have, for example, seen university students referred for consultation whose path to my office began with their request to change their major sequence from history to English. The request led to a series of guidance interviews and a referral to the bureau of tests and measurements. A series of aptitude tests led to a projective battery and a series of personality profiles. The student then heard the verdict that although there was nothing to be alarmed about, some of the test material definitely indicated a psychiatric consultation. Now I have been a psychiatrist for almost fifteen years and I have had a great many interviews concerning a variety of problems but I still don't know what to do when I ask a patient why he came to see me and he responds, "I want to change my major from history to English." This is tossing the client to the wolves.

I have also had experiences in which my examination confirmed the opinion of the guidance department that a given student could not benefit from further education. The examination also elicited clinical support of the psychological battery and the social history and, accordingly, the boy was excused from regular attendance by exemption. Having served in this capacity, however, my name and telephone listing were made available and I was left to explain to the irate parents why I personally expelled their son from school. Administration, it seems, had assumed the position that the boy was more than welcome but the psychiatric recommendation precluded the possibility of readmission. This is throwing the consultant to the wolves and, I might add, makes for poor staff relationships.

What I am afraid I am taking too long to say is that teachers, guidance counselors, school social workers, psychologists, and psychiatrists should be working together instead of working side by side and competing for the larger share of influence in the management of a specific case.

REFERENCES

1. Hatch, Raymond and Stefflre, Buford. *Administration of guidance services.* Englewood Cliffs, New Jersey: Prentice-Hall, Inc., 1958.
2. Arbuckle, Dugald S. *Guidance and counseling in the classroom.* Boston: Allyn and Bacon, Inc., 1957.
3. Miller, Frank W. *Guidance principles and services.* Columbus, Ohio: Charles E. Merrill Books, Inc., 1961.

ADDITIONAL READING

Bier, W. C. (ed.). *The adolescent: his search for understanding.* New York: Fordham Univ. Press, 1963.
Brammer, L. M. and Shostrom, E. L. *Therapeutic psychology: fundamentals of counseling and psychotherapy.* Englewood Cliffs, N.J.: Prentice-Hall, 1960.
Haring, P. *Educating emotionally disturbed children.* New York: McGraw-Hill, 1962.

Josselyn, I. *The happy child*. New York: Random House, 1955.

Krugmans, E. (ed.). *Orthopsychiatry and the school*. New York: Amer. Ortho-psych. Assoc., 1958.

Lorand, S. *Adolescents, a psycho-analytical approach*. New York, Harper, 1961.

Masserman, J. *Dynamic psychiatry*. Philadelphia: W. B. Saunders Co., 1946.

Mullahy, P. *The study of inter-personal relations*. New York: Grove, 1957.

Richards, T. *Modern clinical psychology*. New York: McGraw-Hill, 1946.

Reik, T. *Listening with the third ear*. New York: Grove, 1948.

Roeber, E. C. *The school counselor*. Washington, D.C.: The Center for Applied Research in Education, Inc., 1963.

Snoeck, A., S.J. *Confession and pastoral psychology*. Westminster, Md: Newman, 1961.

Snoeck, A., S.J. *Confession and psychoanalysis*. Westminster, Md.: Newman, 1964.

Stern, K. *The third revolution, a study of psychiatry and religion*. New York: Harcourt, 1954.

Thorne, F. *Principles of personality counseling*. Brandon, Vermont: Journal of Clinical Psychology, 1950.

Vandervelt, J. M. and Odenwald, R. P. *Psychiatry and Catholicism*. New York: McGraw-Hill, 1957 (2nd ed.).

White, R. *The abnormal personality*. New York: Ronald Press, 1956 (2nd ed.).

Cf. issues of:

American Journal of Orthopsychiatry. This journal is devoted to the collaborative approach of psychiatrists, psychologists, psychiatric social workers and other behavioral sciences in the study and treatment of human behavior.

Robert J. McNamara, S.J.

is Assistant Professor of Sociology, Fordham University. He was awarded B.A. and M.A. degrees at St. Louis University, completed his theological studies at Woodstock College, and received a Ph.D. degree at Cornell University. He is a member of the American Sociological Association and the American Catholic Sociological Association. He is also a member of the editorial board of Sociological Analysis, *the journal of the American Catholic Sociological Society. He was a contributor to* Marriage, A Psychological and Moral Approach *(ed. W. C. Bier, S.J.). Titles of recent journal articles written by Fr. McNamara include: "Intellectual Values and Instrumental Religion," "Intellectual Values: Campus and Seminary," and "Higher Education and American Catholicism."*

Guidance and Sociology

At this point in the general inquiry into the relationships between guidance and the various disciplines which fall under the general heading of the social sciences, we shall try to answer one question and one question only. It is this: how can sociology and the sociologist help guidance personnel—i.e., the people responsible for helping students to make the choices which are best for them—whether the choice be vocational, occupational, educational, or moral?

The question is a large one, and I shall try to make it more manageable by breaking it down into two smaller, but still uncomfortably large, questions. First, is there a sort of sociological

57

way of thinking—a sociological habit of thought or method of approaching the social realities—which may aid the counselor as he helps the counselee make his choices? Second, are there any social data, in the form of empirical generalizations, uncovered by the sociologists which the counselor can use as definite guidelines as he frames his advice to those who seek it? In contrast to usual procedure, we shall deal with the first question first.

If the counselor's job is to help the student make the proper choices—choices which must be the student's own—then he is first of all a liberator and only secondarily a guider. As far as possible—which is frequently not very far—he must free the student from attitudes and values which inhibit the student's range of choice. Of course, the counselor cannot take on this job alone, for one principal purpose of liberal education is to do precisely that. But the counselor is frequently in the position where he must bring all the benefits of the student's previous education to bear as he makes his choices. That is why the sociological habit of thought can be invaluable to the counselor. For it is the task of the sociologist to identify cultural values, relate them to what is usually considered his most proper object of study, social structures, and then, together with the social psychologist and the psychologist, to see how these influences merge within the individual human personality.

It is not for me to discuss the various types of testing which are so important for the counselor: personality, educational, and vocational. It is up to the counselor to link the results of such testing to social structure and patterned cultural values with which the student lives and which he makes his own.

Let me make these categories of social structure, cultural values, and personality more explicit. For the behavioral scientist, personality is at least a whole series of related traits, or characteristics, which have been built up over time by a pattern of action which is essentially a response pattern. The individual, with his unique biological inheritance, including a kind of biological temperament, responds from early infancy to the demands, requests, and necessities of his environmental situation. His parents, the rest of his family, later his playmates, friends, teachers, occupational group, all *expect* him to respond within the pattern of their values and norms. Thus we have no mechanical operation, but a rather freewheeling series of adjustments and innovations which go on all through life. Through this process the personality is formed. About this we shall say no more, but pass on to what is proper to sociology. For help in the area of personality the guidance official must turn to those social psychologists again.

Social structures are just what their name says they are. They are edifices which men in society raise so that together they can accomplish their human goals and together express and satisfy their human needs. The complexity of these structures makes the complex structure of the Empire State building, the Narrows-Verrazano bridge, or even the mysterious atom, seem like a simple jigsaw puzzle. Just to take a glance at their complexity in modern society, consider the plight of the poor helpless infant (forgetting for the moment the plight of the parents who are at the mercy of this unthinking tyrant). His only awareness of the world around him at first is that there is something out there which is apparently made to satisfy him—and if it does not, he shrieks his discomfort. As time goes on, he begins to recognize the *quid pro quo* principle. Unless he cooperates, i.e., unless he starts living up to the expectations of that outside world and its main representative—in our culture, his mother— he is just not going to be satisfied but will be punished instead. As more time goes on he must live up to more and more of these expectations. It is always a struggle, for instance, to convince him of the purpose of a bathroom and how he is to contribute to it; then that other things have their place, which teaches him the difference between the closet and the living room floor; then that there are jobs that he *can and therefore should* do.

(My younger brother's job at about age four and for some years thereafter was to empty the house scrapbaskets. He really never could see why he should empty other people's scrapbaskets when he would have much preferred to serve us all by driving the family car. Fortunately, despite repeated effort, he never succeeded in getting the old Buick going. But even now, at the age of 33 or so, if there is a steering wheel within 10 miles, you will find him behind it. This could be interpreted as a drive for dominance with all sorts of juicy libidinal over- and under-tones, but I think he is only escaping from scrapbaskets—sub-consciously, of course.)

The process of "can and therefore should" goes on for quite a while. A child *can* start to play with other children; therefore he *should,* or else he is not "normal." He *can* go to school and start to learn his three R's; therefore he should. He *can* go to college, sometimes only in the sense that his parents can pay his way; therefore he should, if only in the eyes of his misguided parents.

The point behind all this complexity is straightforward. Social structures are complex series of relationships all based on one key word: *expectations*—a concept analogous to the "can and therefore should" law of childhood. Notice that this means that we all have roles to play, some more or less freely chosen, others not freely chosen at all. We are *expected* to do certain things, perform certain actions. Our roles coincide with what others expect of us.

There is not an exact one-to-one correspondence here, but there is a close one. Whenever you wish to subvert the social structure, any time you wish to "stop the action," just do the un-expected. This is recognized as a standard military principle in wartime, but think of the delightful havoc you could wreak in peacetime if you went about doing the unexpected. Suppose a high school principal, at a morning assembly on an ordinary Monday, simply announced that there would be no school for three weeks. A thousand parents would jam the switchboard with phone calls, teachers would fume at time lost (or at least rail at the lack of communication between administration and faculty), and the principal would be removed. Or suppose 50 percent of all Long Island husbands and fathers simply did not come home after a hard day at the office in Manhattan; suppose they substituted a jet to Los Angeles for the Long Island Railroad commuter train. They would certainly stop the action. Social structures would collapse all along Long Island: familial, occupational, economic, and political.

There is one situation in which the unexpected is expected to happen, and it is worth considering. Turn on your television set to a comedy show, go to a movie comedy, or read a novel intended to be hilarious. If you can predict the outcome, or at least most of the situations and lines, it is a poor comedy and you will not find yourself laughing. For comedy consists in putting two incongruous things together which no one has ever put together in quite the same way before. They are not *expected* to be found together, and when we find them together, we laugh. We just do not take comedy seriously. It might be noted that the man who entertains us is rarely the man who leads us. We just do not take him seriously. He is the court jester, not the king.

This insight about "can and therefore should" as well as the complementarity of expectations and roles is tremendously important for understanding social structures. All those social structures which we call "institutions" are in reality a series of expectations and roles which a society considers so important for the development of its members and its own preservation that very heavy penalties are applied to those who do not play their expected institutional roles. Marriage is such a structure and such an institution. In our society, a man is expected to have only one wife; formerly one for life, now at least only one at a time. If he has two, he has committed bigamy, a violation of his expected monogamous role, and he goes to jail. If he does not support his wife and the children he has fathered, he is considered a bum by society and can be hauled into court. He has not done the expected. Our whole series of economic institutions are nothing but a web of expectations expressed legally in the law of contract. If a man or a corporation contracts for a job and does not perform it, he is liable at least to civil suit and can go to jail. The law of contract is so ironbound that we have had to build escape hatches in it: limited liability for those owning stock in a corporation, as well as the law of bankruptcy for individuals. The purpose of the latter is to get a man out from under financial obligations, or expectations, which he cannot possibly fulfill.

We could continue in this vein for a long time. I am insisting on it because it is a very important part of the sociological habit of mind, a habit which I think a counselor should have. When a youngster is about to make a choice, be it educational, vocational, or occupational, the counselor must help him to see all the expectations which society has for those who choose to play the role he is taking upon himself. The question then becomes: can he fulfill those expectations?

VALUES AND NORMS

There is, however, another important half of the sociological habit of mind to which we must now turn. After the possibility of someone's playing a certain role, fulfilling certain expectations, has been handled—and I do not mean that "after" in a temporal sense necessarily—the next question must be: why *should* he fulfill them? With this question we come to the problem of values and norms.

Here we are in an area which is difficult to analyze, but which the sociologist must analyze, and which the counselor must analyze as he does his job. I am not speaking merely of moral values and moral norms. Indeed, a "traditional" set of moral norms, stiffly applied, can be a handicap to the counselor, for they may shift the counselor's attention to what the counselor thinks the student *should* see from what the student actually *does* see—always a dangerous process which may turn the interview into an effort to persuade or to "lay down the law" rather than help it to be what it should be: the effort to liberate and then to guide. Thus if the counselor places primary value on high school as a time to learn, with a moral obligation not to waste time, and the student sees it as a period of fun and games, they will pass each other right by, the values of each untouched by the other.

By the term "value" sociologists usually mean criterion, or

standard, according to which things are judged good or bad in any sense, moral, esthetic, or even cognitive. A value, therefore, is that which makes a goal a goal. It justifies something as worth being sought. Norms, on the other hand, are the socially approved ways of getting to those goals. Let me mention a general, and perhaps overworked, American example. Financial success is a generally approved American goal, supported by the values of prestige, power, security, and personal freedom. The most approved ways of getting there are through business and the professions. Both of these avenues call for much previous education, at least nowadays. When these two thruways, and their educational feed roads, are blocked or made quite difficult for individuals or groups, we observe the phenomena either of illegitimate enterprise dominated by the discriminated-against group, or the appearance of many members of the group in enterprises with which less prestige is associated but which pay great rewards to the few at the top. Thus, if you watch TV's *Untouchables*, you get the idea that almost all Prohibition criminals were Italian. It just so happened that Prohibition offered a wonderful, illegitimate way to make money to the latest immigrant group of that era—and they were Italians. The prizefight ring is now dominated by colored Americans, but in the recent past the champions were Italians and before that they were Irish. Baseball rosters now list many Spanish-American names and boast many Negro players. Twenty years ago both were absent from the rosters. This is an old, old American story. When the ways of securing financial and occupational success upon which society places most prestige and in which there is most chance of attaining American goals are out of the reach of minority groups, the groups will find other ways of getting there, either illegitimate or at least less prestigious.

As far as the question of values and norms is concerned, the application is clear. If the minority group does accept the values and goals of the dominant society, as it usually does, and if they are excluded from the means of access to those goals which are the *normal* means, as they usually are, then they will find means which are not so normal—in the double sense of being either unusual or illegitimate.

This large sociological view of values and norms can be a help to the counselor when, as he must, he focuses on the individual student. Alerted by the general cultural picture, the counselor must be able to cut through to the values and to the norms held by the individual. Here he is really practicing his important art, for here he must let the student tell him, in the groping, inarticulate way which most students have, what he really does value and why. When his reasons for holding them are inadequate, or when the values he holds are superficial reflections of the general culture, or when he is holding on to contradictory values, the student must be led to discover the inadequacy, the contradiction, or the superficiality for himself. A few examples, culled from cross-cultural study, of values and norms and their relationships may bring out just the kind of thing that the student must see if he is to open his eyes to the fact that his own values and norms are not to be taken for granted as being uniquely true and unquestionably good.

A century or so ago in Japan the coming of age of the young samurai boy—i.e., the boy who belonged to the warrior nobility (and there was no other nobility) —was marked by strapping the samurai sword onto his belt. He had attained his manhood and this was society's recognition of it as well as his own expression of it. Today, the young man living in Harlem or New York's lower east side who starts to carry a switchblade to express his own fledgling manhood is not nearly so well received by society. But the value is the same; it is the expression of it, or the norm, which has changed. The wonderful family spirit still existing among most members of Italian-American families used to be expressed in the United States by the young man's going to work at the first opportunity so that he could contribute to the family. But precisely by making such a contribution, the sons cut themselves off from further education and so delayed their cultural acceptance by American society. The whole Catholic educational system from kindergarten to graduate school, at least until after World War II, was primarily geared to protect the faith of the children of the Catholic immigrant in an alien culture. This was a fine value, but it cut the Catholic off from the mainstream of American intellectual life. The youngster of today is caught between the value of security as expressed in the steady dating pattern, and the values of gregariousness and educational advancement, still strong in America. He must recognize this conflict, but normally he will not unless he is guided to do so. The "moral law" and "danger to faith and morals" advice rarely does much good. But the inherent contradiction between opposing values which he does in fact hold can be made the object of his conscious reflection.

Values can act in another way. They can prevent the value holder from seeing what is right under his nose. Let me take an example from a current development which Andrew Greeley has dubbed the "New Breed." For Fr. Greeley, the New Breed are concerned with "integrity and honesty," so much so that they cannot be political or even diplomatic. They are neither "flexible" nor "gradualist" in their demand for change.

They are a paradoxical bunch, supremely self-confident, yet anxious and restless; they are organizationally efficient and yet often diplomatically tactless; they are eager to engage in dialogue and yet frequently inarticulate in what they want to say; they are without ideology and yet insistent on freedom; they are generous with the poor and suffering and terribly harsh in their judgment on their elders and superiors; they are ecumenical to the core and yet terribly parochial in their tastes and fashions; they want desperately to love but are not sure that they know how to love. They want to scale the heights yet are mired in the foothills (*America,* May 24, 1964, pp. 706-9).

To place Fr. Greeley's idea of the New Breed in the context of values and norms, I would define them as a group, usually although not necessarily young in age, who have taken as their own two values: personalism and criticism. Their personalism places an accent on personal activism and self-fulfillment through idealistic activity in causes of social, religious, or intellectual importance. Their value of criticism leads them to be forthright, to say the least, in declaring that the generation ahead of them has not been all that it should be. They can be embarrassingly accurate in pinpointing the shortcomings of their elders.

Now personalism and criticism can be very good things. When personalism finds its expression in the Peace Corps or the Papal Volunteers, in real activity for political reform, in dedication to civil rights, it is very good indeed, and we call it a norm or a means in which this value is legitimately expressed. In our old-fashioned way we might even call these expressions of personalism virtues. But it can emerge as a vice only too easily. When it places the accent on exclusively selfish "self-fulfillment" without any real effort to measure up to norms outside the self which are already embedded in existing institutions, when it emerges in activity which effectively ranks juvenile "kicks" over personal rights of the self or of others, or over property rights, then it is most certainly a vice—an illegitimate norm or means of expressing a value which *could* have emerged as a virtue.

The same holds true of the value of criticism. When it emerges in practice as toughness of mind, independence of judgment, or spirit of inquiry rather than overeasy acceptance of past formulations, then it is quite good indeed. It is a virtue. We need more of it, for no institutionalized way of doing things is ever final. But when it emerges as a total rejection of all authority, or even as a prejudice against all holders of authority simply because they hold authority, then it is indeed a vice.

We can give the New Breed something, however, if we are more patient than our forebears were with us and rely less on authority than was done by our elders. This brings me back to the reason for which I mentioned the New Breed in the first place. Their values of personalism and criticism can obscure other values for them, so that they see neither these other values nor their expressions. If we ourselves are convinced that diplomacy is a value we can make them aware of it. The same holds for a reasonable amount of respect for authority, articulateness, prudence, and even justice. They can see these values if they are exposed to them. They can talk themselves into these values if we just do not argue with these boys and girls, these men and women of the New Breed.

GUIDANCE AND SOCIOLOGY

Let me say, parenthetically, that there is one certainly good result of all this, whether the values of personalism and criticism emerge as virtues or vices, for all teachers, counselors, and administrators. We cannot count any longer on even an external acceptance of what we say, no matter how idiotic one's sayings may sometimes be. None of us is always right, and all of us are occasionally idiots. We find out more quickly nowadays just when we are idiots.

EMPIRICAL GENERALIZATIONS

This section of the present paper will try to draw together a few well founded generalizations culled from recent efforts by sociologists to try and get at the facts. The areas from which they are drawn are those which seem likely to be of more than passing interest to guidance officials and counselors, particularly those in Catholic schools.

RELIGION AND CHOICE OF COLLEGE

"Danger to the faith" is widely used as a reason for not going to a non-Catholic college while spiritual and moral—as well as intellectual—growth in the faith is used as a reason for going to a Catholic college. The implications, then, are: a) that Catholics who go to non-Catholic colleges run great risk of apostasy; b) that they will be less likely to practice their religion; c) that they may cease to hold some Catholic interpretations of the moral law; d) that they will not grow in appreciation of their faith. What evidence do we have to back up these presumptions? Not much. Let us examine each in turn.

Apostasy at the Nonsectarian College. This so-called danger is almost non-existent. A national study of the June, 1961 college graduates was done by the National Opinion Research Center at the University of Chicago, and the religious data gathered by the Center were analyzed by Andrew Greeley, now a Senior Study Director at NORC (1964). This analysis revealed that among the Catholic seniors who had attended Catholic high school and

67

college, 1 percent were apostates; that among those who attended Catholic college only, 3 percent were apostates; that among those who went to Catholic high schools and nonsectarian colleges, 9 percent were apostates; that among those who went neither to Catholic high school nor to Catholic college, 18 percent were apostates. Even these small differences cannot be attributed directly to the colleges or to the high schools, because the students may not have been practicing Catholics before they got to the high school or to the college. Danger of apostasy, therefore, is hardly a factor to be taken into consideration when giving advice to the graduate of a Catholic high school, unless he or she gives definite signs that he is already notably weak in the practice of religion.

Practice of Religion at Nonsectarian Colleges. Ninety-five percent of the Catholic seniors who had a Catholic high school and college education attend Mass regularly; 93 percent of those do so who had Catholic college education only; 85 percent of those who went to a Catholic high school but to a nonsectarian college; 72 percent of those who went to non-Catholic high school and college. But, among this latter group, of those who still consider themselves Catholics, "the percent of those who do not go to Mass regularly is little different from other groups. Approximately seven-eighths of the all non-Catholic education group who are still Catholics are regular churchgoers, as are more than nine-tenths of those who went to Catholic high school only but were still Catholics at graduation from college" (Greeley, p. 83). Notice that this is higher than the national average for Mass attendance of all Catholics. Therefore the danger of becoming a non-practicing Catholic cannot be taken as a *general* criterion for attending or not attending a nonsectarian college.

Official Catholic Beliefs. There is some evidence which suggests that on particular issues like sexual morality, divorce, and contraception, many Catholics on nonsectarian campuses depart from the official Catholic positions, at least while they are in college, if—and this is a big "if"—virtually all their classmates hold opinions on these issues which are different from official Catholic teaching. Thus, among the Catholic seniors on the Cornell and the Columbia campuses in the years 1961 and 1962, respectively, only one-third hold that "heavy necking" is wrong, and only one-half hold that premarital sexual relations between those engaged to be married are wrong. Three-quarters and seven-eighths of the Fordham and the Notre Dame seniors in those same two years thought that the two types of behavior were wrong. But it would be risky to generalize from such data, for Columbia and Cornell are both high prestige institutions, and differences like these always show up more strongly at high prestige colleges than at other colleges. On the other hand, strong evidence indicates that the nonsectarian campus seniors, including Catholics, take a much more serious view of cheating, and actually cheat less, than do the seniors on the Catholic campuses (McNamara, 1963).

Appreciation of Religious Faith. This is an area in which it is extraordinarily difficult to secure reliable data. We know that the nonsectarian college experience leaves about half of the students placing the same value on religious faith as they placed on it when they started college (Jacob, 1957, p. 21). Of the remaining half, approximately one-third value religion less, and two-thirds value it more—although at the prestige colleges the percentages are somewhat less favorable toward religion. Considerably more of the Catholics—as opposed to the non-Catholics —on the nonsectarian campuses say that they value religion more since entering college. On the Catholic college campuses, if we may take Fordham and Notre Dame as representative institutions, well over half of the seniors say that they value religion more since entering college, one-third are unchanged in their evaluation, and only a small group, about 10 percent, say that they value religion less.*

There is one definite phenomenon which can be attributed to the Catholic college. A relatively very large proportion of the Catholic graduates of Catholic colleges, no matter what type of secondary school they attended, expect that religious beliefs and

* This data is based on the study, *The Interplay of Intellectual and Religious Values.* See McNamara, 1963.

activities will be one of their major areas of life satisfaction. This interesting fact turns up in both the NORC study and the Fordham-Notre Dame-Columbia-Cornell study referred to above.

The meaning of these general statements must be carefully checked out, as we continue our efforts to discover just what the religious impact of the college and high school really is. One should not jump to the conclusion that this general attitude favorable to religion is the result of the theology or religion curriculum, although we hope that it is. It may be due to the general Catholic atmosphere of the campus, or to the religious background of most of the students, to mention just two possibilities. For a counselor to make the high school graduates' main motive for attending a Catholic college the theological and the philosophical courses offered by the college is at times unwise, inviting a boomerang effect. This motivation places the department of theology particularly, but also of philosophy, in a vulnerable position. One insipid sociology course, for example, causes no cosmic reaction among college students. But a required course in theology, particularly in freshman or sophomore year, which is somewhat less than successful, can destroy the reason that a student had for coming to the college. His expectations should not be raised too high, for, after all, theology and philosophy are academic disciplines subject to all the pitfalls which beset any college course.

The purpose of this section has not been to dissuade counselors from advising young men and women to attend Catholic colleges. The evidence indicates, at least provisionally, that if they do go to Catholic as opposed to non-Catholic colleges, they will be *more likely* to emerge with a greater appreciation of religious faith and with a higher expectation of the part that their religion will play in their lives after college. The evidence also indicates that there is little likelihood of their "losing the faith" or becoming non-practicing Catholics while on the campuses of America's nonsectarian colleges.

Now we must turn to the question of religious attitudes. There is considerable evidence that religious attitudes are linked in complex ways to subjects which are of considerable interest to the educator and the counselor.

RELIGIOUS ATTITUDES

One proposition—namely, that Catholics and Catholic colleges are less "intellectual" than are non-Catholics and nonsectarian colleges—must now be laid to rest. At one time (before World War II) it was true as far as we can tell from the available evidence concerning the Catholic Church in America (Ellis, 1956; O'Dea, 1958). But nowadays the same type of evidence shows us that the situation has changed. To mention just a bit of this post-World War II evidence: as a matter of *fact*, Catholics are going to graduate school in the pure arts and sciences, and are staying in such graduate schools, in just the same—or even slightly higher—proportions as their non-Catholic colleagues; the graduates of Catholic colleges are doing exactly the same; Catholic universities are increasing their Ph.D. awards at a rate higher than that of all other American universities; the number of Catholic college graduates who subsequently earn the Ph.D. is increasing at a higher rate than is the number of graduates of all other American colleges (Greeley, 1963; McNamara, 1965).

All this, however, does not mean that religious attitudes are unrelated to intellectual values. Among the graduates of Fordham (1961) and Notre Dame (1962), those whose attitude toward their religion was "instrumental" were far less likely to be interested in intellectual values than those whose religious attitude was not instrumental. This statement calls for some explanation.

We have known for some time that churchgoers are more likely to manifest prejudice toward minority groups than the unchurched are. But we also know that some churchgoers are far less prejudiced, as a group, than are most Americans. We further know that this presence or absence of prejudice is correlated with the attitude the churchgoers have toward their religion: if their church and religion are primarily instruments which they use for social prestige, for psychic security, or for moral support, then they manifest a high degree of prejudice; but if their church and religion are primarily ways in which they manifest their devotion to God and to their fellow men, then they manifest a low degree of prejudice (Allport, pp. 420-22).

The same affinity appears when the relationship between Catholics and intellectual values is scrutinized. Catholic college seniors whose religious attitude can be termed "instrumental" are far less interested in going to graduate school in the pure arts and sciences, have much less interest in the invention and in the communication of knowledge, and are more inclined to use prestige and monetary rewards as criteria for their occupational choices than is the case with those whose religious attitude is not instrumental. Thus, if the Catholic looks to his religion *primarily* as a moral guide, to prayer *primarily* as a means of peace of soul or adjustment to the universe, to God primarily as a problem solver, then he is less likely to be interested in intellectual values than is the Catholic who looks to his religion and prayer primarily as a means of expressing love, honor and gratitude to the God on whom he believes he is dependent. In the former case, the believer is using prayer and God primarily as instruments— tools—for his own satisfaction, subverting the order in which he says he believes; in the latter case, he is not.

The implication of these empirically-established relationships is simply this: an instrumental religious attitude inhibits intellectual interests, or is at least positively associated with lower intellectual interests. The instrumental religious attitude builds a fence around the person, preventing him from seeing the world as it is, keeping him within a restricted area. The great truths of man and his universe have less appeal to him and the desire to play a role in the discovery of still unknown or only partially known truths is less compelling. The instrumentally religious man uses religion to shield himself from the universe; the genuinely religious man uses it to relate himself to it (McNamara, 1964).

To recognize the "instrumental syndrome" and to attempt to break it down is surely the task of the educator and the counselor. Doubtless, there is some instrumentalism in all of us. That fact may help us to recognize when there is too much of it.

It is interesting to note that for a culture—in particular, the culture of the nonsectarian college campus—within which traditional religious beliefs are not so pervasive and intense as they are on the Catholic college campus, there is another set of attitudes and values which are correlated with lessened intellectual interests. They are connected with a set of beliefs which I call the American democratic ideology: belief in the dignity of the human person, in the quality of man, in man's uniqueness in the animal kingdom. These beliefs and values are shared by all, or virtually all, on the nonsectarian college campus. But there are those who apply them less widely than others—i.e., there are those who tend to restrict, for some individuals or groups, the exercise of the rights which they claim for themselves. As in the case of the instrumental religious attitude, we find that this restrictivism is associated with what we made the villain of the piece when dealing with religious attitudes: a lack of open-mindedness to the problems and mysteries of man and his universe, and, by inference, a readiness to make prejudiced statements. Thus, the man who is quick to condemn conscientious objectors as cowards, to demand that labor unions be restricted in their existence as associations, to deny a U.S. responsibility for helping less developed countries, to insist that unwholesome religions (whatever that may mean) be suppressed—this man is far less likely to place high value on intellectual interests (McNamara, 1963).

CONCLUSION

The meaning of all this for the art of guidance is, I hope, fairly clear. People, it seems, can go through the whole educational process without recognizing and reflecting upon the set of cultural values in which they were reared and which they have made their own. The task of education, at least of secondary and of higher education, is to make these values explicit, and then lead the student to make choices which are as conscious, as well informed, and as wise as possible. For the counselor particularly, and we all act as counselors, the problem is one of focusing the

73

student's attention on all that he has learned and observed as he makes his important choices. To do this the student must see his own background, his own cultural values and attitudes as "givens"—call them the "independent variables." These variables affect us all differently, so there are "intervening variables," the personal attitudes of the individual student as he is. Both of these types of variables, taken together, give the person an image of himself. Knowing his own image, the student must make his choices. As counselors, we must make these variables as clearly understood and as relevant as possible to the individual human being whom we are trying to help. Sociology, I hope, is helpful.

REFERENCES

Allport, Gordon. *The nature of prejudice.* New York: Doubleday Anchor Books, 1958. Pp. 420-22.

Ellis, John Tracy. *American Catholics and the intellectual life.* Chicago: Heritage Foundation, 1956.

Greeley, Andrew M. *Religion and career.* New York: Sheed & Ward, 1963. Esp. pp. 73-86.

Jacob, Philip E. *Changing values in college.* New York: Harper, 1957.

McNamara, R. J. "The interplay of intellectual and religious values" (unpublished doctoral dissertation, Cornell Univer., 1963). Chap. VI.

McNamara, R. J. Intellectual values and instrumental religion. *Sociolog. Anal.,* Summer, 1964.

McNamara, R. J. "Catholics in academia" in *American Catholic Church in transition,* ed. by M. Schlitz and A. Greeley. New York: John Wiley, 1965.

O'Dea, Thomas F. *American Catholic Dilemma: an inquiry into the intellectual life.* New York: Sheed & Ward, 1958.

ADDITIONAL READING

Bell, R. (ed.). *The sociology of education, a sourcebook.* Homewood, Ill.: Dorsey Press, 1962.

Borow, H. (ed.). *Man in a world at work.* Boston: Houghton Mifflin, 1964.

Caplow, T. *The sociology of work.* Minneapolis: Univ. of Minnesota Press, 1954.

Charters, W. W. *Readings in the social psychology of education.* Boston: Allyn & Bacon, 1963.

Cook, E. *A sociological approach to education.* New York: McGraw-Hill, 1950.
Halsey, A. H. (ed.). *Education, economy and society; readings in the sociology of education.* Glencoe, Ill.: Free Press, 1961.
Havighurst, R. *Society and education.* Boston: Allyn & Bacon, 1962.
Levenstein, A. *Why people work.* Tarrytown, N.Y.: Collier, 1962.
Miller, C. H. *Foundations of guidance.* New York: Harper & Row, 1961.
Montagu-Ashley, M. F. *On being human.* New York: Schuman, 1950.
Moreno, J. L. *The sociometry reader.* Glencoe, Ill.: Free Press, 1960.
Riesman, D. *The lonely crowd, a study of the changing American culture.* New Haven: Yale University Press, 1956.
Riezler, K. *Man mutable and immutable, the fundamental structure of social life.* Chicago: Regnery, 1950.
Rosenberg, M. *Occupations and values.* Glencoe, Ill.: Free Press, 1957.
Warner, W. L. *Who shall be educated?* New York: Harper, 1954.

Cf. issues of:

Behavioral Science. This interdisciplinary journal is "of wider scope than any single discipline and makes its pages available to representatives of any field—the humanities, the social sciences, the biological and medical sciences, and the physical sciences—to discuss theory concerning behavior, and empirical studies clearly oriented to such theory."

Elizabeth M. Eddy, Ph.D.

*is Project Director of Research in Project
TRUE (Teacher Resources for Urban Education), Hunter College. This project involves anthropological and sociological research in urban schools. She was awarded
the B.A. degree by Wellesley, an M.A. by
Teachers College, and the Ph.D. in social
psychology from Columbia University. Formerly she was assistant project Director, New
York School of Social Work, and Director of
Education at several Episcopalian parishes
in this country. Among her many professional memberships are the following: the
Society for Applied Anthropology, of which
she is a fellow; the American Anthropological Association, the American Psychological
Association, and the American Association
for the Advancement of Science. Her journal
publications include: "Rites of Passage in a
Total Institution," and "Attitudes towards
Desegregation among Southern Students on
a Northern Campus."*

Anthropology and Guidance

The recent concern of guidance counselors in re-examining
their work and their relationship to clients, the educational system and society is of interest to social scientists who find themselves being requested to provide new insights to guidance practitioners or to work with them in the solution of their professional problems. This upsurge of curiosity about the social
sciences on the part of guidance counselors reflects a more widespread movement among educators in general to use the findings
and abilities of social scientists. Although social scientists have

long worked in governmental, industrial, and medical settings, their entrance into educational institutions is considerably more recent and rare but currently expanding rapidly.

The discovery of the social sciences on the part of educators may be new, but the social sciences have long focused attention on educational processes and on those means whereby a society appraises individual strengths and limitations and accordingly provides people with different roles in society. In American society the role of the school as a mechanism of social differentiation has been described by sociologists, and a recent study has delineated the role of guidance counselors as educational decision-makers who have considerable influence in advancing some groups of students and holding others back (Cicourel & Kitsuse, 1963). Similarly, psychologists have devoted much careful research to social influences on test results and have demonstrated the way in which testing favors selected segments of our population. For years anthropologists have studied the processes by which one generation transmits its culture to the next generation and trains the young in the knowledge and skills necessary for cultural survival. Because so much of its work has been done in other cultures, however, the contribution of anthropology to an understanding of our own society is more obscure to the layman than is the application of sociology or psychology, and there is a need to demonstrate the relevance of anthropology for contemporary American educational problems. This paper represents an attempt in this direction and will begin with a brief summary of some aspects of American education deemed to be important by anthropologists and will then turn to a consideration of anthropological insights into the process of guidance (Henry, 1963; Kimball & McClellan, 1962; Spindler, 1963).

ENVIRONMENTAL FACTORS IN AMERICAN EDUCATION

In considering the application of anthropological studies to contemporary American education, one must of course be aware of the differences between small, primitive, non-literate societies and our own highly developed technological society. In the former societies, children learn what they need to know in order to be incorporated into the society as adults, outside of a formally organized educational structure. Relatives and other adults teach the child within the setting of family and community life except in those instances where children or young adolescents may be segregated for periods of time in preparation for initiation rites or to learn highly specialized adult roles. In the main, primitive societies are noteworthy for the continuity between generations.

In contrast to primitive societies, American society largely enforces the segregation of American children and youth into the formal age-graded institution of the modern school and emphasizes the discontinuity between generations. Thus we deliberately aim to "turn the child of the peasant into a clerk, of the farmer into a lawyer, of the Italian immigrant into an American, of the illiterate into the literate" (Mead, 1943). Education entails a separation from the parental womb and an induction and incorporation into the vast bureaucratic structure of the modern educational enterprise. To educate the young, we commission a group of civil servants paid and licensed by the government and equipped with an increasingly standardized curriculum built around our perception of the age characteristics of children in particular grades and those things which we feel they should know before another year passes by. The process of schooling is one in which the child moves from his present status as a child who leaves home on a partial basis to an adult who leaves home completely and participates in the corporation or bureaucratic life so common to the contemporary American scene. From attending kindergarten for half a day, the child moves to attending college on a full-time basis and ideally living away from home on a college campus. Thus the educational organization demands more and more of a child's life, energy, and time and provides a preparation for the later demands of job and family.

The relationship between formal education and occupational roles is increasingly strong in American society and will continue to grow as specialization increases and unskilled tasks become automatic. Even a cursory examination of the available statistics clearly shows a high correlation between levels of education attained and the type of work pursued. The uneducated and those with little education comprise a goodly portion of those who must be cared for by welfare agencies. Thus in 1958, among the nearly eight million multiple-person families whose heads had less than eight years of elementary education, approximately two-thirds lived in poverty and subsisted on less than $4000 per year. More than one-third had incomes under $2000. On the other hand, among the four million families whose heads had completed four years of college or more, less than one-tenth lived in poverty and approximately seventy-five percent had incomes of $6000 or more. To drop out of school prematurely today is to drop out of adult work roles in our society which is less and less able to provide meaningful employment for the non-educated (Conference on Economic Progress, 1962, p. 61).

Because contemporary American schools are so intimately related to the world of work, they are largely recruitment and training grounds for occupational roles. The selection of children for particular schools and colleges and specific programs within the educational institution is essentially a selection for their future place in the labor market. This may be seen in our clear emphasis on selecting the academically talented early, segregating them in special classses, and preparing them for the better colleges and universities. The formal deliberate and long educational program by means of which we meet the needs of our complex society is quite different from the informal types of education which occur in the family, peer group and local communities of all societies. It is also different from the one-room schoolhouses of our forebears.

For a quick overview of what has happened to American society in the past century, one has only to contrast the McGuffey Readers with the Dick and Jane Series of readers or their equivalents. The McGuffey Readers staunchly upheld Victorian morality and described the temptations, trials, and duties to which all persons are subject as human beings. Children are not excluded from the adult realities of death nor the consequences of doing one's duty. Embedded in Protestant Christianity the readers attempt to relate the young not only to their local farms and towns but also to the nation, Western civilization and even to God Himself.

In contrast, the Dick and Jane readers introduce the child solely to the contemporary world of suburban family, selected fairy tales and anthropomorphic stories about animals. The families portrayed are nuclear middle-class, child-centered families in which other relatives play a secondary role, the father works in a downtown office and the mother keeps house while the children attend school. Family solidarity is not built around work but rather the family is brought together by means of shared leisure time activities. Adults have easy friendly relationships with children, and life is one big series of fun and games, unhaunted by tragedy, sickness, or death. Work is necessary as a way of providing the means for leisure time enjoyment but is kept in the background insofar as possible during the leisure hours. In brief, the Dick and Jane readers describe the Promised Land of Suburbia which has grown up around our cities and make of our countryside a series of sprawling interconnected metropolitan areas rather than isolated small towns and farms widely separated by vast stretches of open land.

The changes in American life from a rural agrarian economy to the modern metropolitan technological age has been accompanied by the growth of our educational system into a huge bureaucracy (Callahan, 1962). Modelled after industry, the school system of today is noteworthy for a supervisory line organization in which decisions made by those at the top are passed down to those at the bottom by means of the printed or spoken word. Within this human organization, pupils are at the bottom in roles comparable to factory laborers, and teachers are just above them in roles comparable to factory foremen. The task of teaching is largely defined as that of initiating work for pupils to do, supervising the work of pupils, passing judgment on it and deciding which pupils have performed well enough so that they may undertake the new work in the next grade on the organizational ladder.

Pupils are carefully trained for their subordinate roles in the human organization known as school. Their physical space is limited and typically confined to the area in front of the teacher and to a specific desk and chair. Physical movement around the classroom is sharply curtailed and there are rules governing the times, if any, during which it is permissible for pupils to initiate action toward the teacher. To be legitimate, pupil initiation of action must be related to classwork, and play or overt expressions of hostility are not tolerated. While they are within the school building, pupils are expected to conform to school regulations laid down by their adult supervisors and infractions of the rules are punished. The role of the school in teaching the proper social behavior to accompany a subordinate role is particularly evident in the slum school where many children are untutored in the social behavior expected by their middle-class elders but it is by no means exclusive in the slum school. Nearly all Americans can testify to at least one experience in which they received a lower academic grade which was not due to the quality of the work done but to a rule infraction.

The bureaucratic definition of the teacher as one who is herself or himself to be supervised insures that she or he teaches the prescribed course in the correct manner. It also curtails the emergence of the teacher as a professional person and is conducive to keeping teachers in comparatively low status positions. As anyone familiar with labor relations might have predicted, it has resulted in the formation of teacher unions in which teachers can unite against their supervisors in a demand for better treatment and more recognition.

The relationship between the type of learning that occurs and the environmental setting in which learning takes place is a matter needing serious study. Anthropologists would and do insist that this is a highly relevant question in America today, and there are indications from other quarters that the factory model of school organization may no longer be appropriate for our needs—if indeed it ever was. Certainly the use of drill and rote techniques is adequate for the memorization of facts to be spewed forth in one or two word answers to objective tests. But there is serious question as to the adequacy of drill and rote in producing persons who can learn to learn in the sense of developing faculties whereby new experiences can be ordered and related to old experiences even if former categories of thought have to be rent asunder in the process.

Writing on this point, Solon T. Kimball notes the following:

. . . the supervisory system, as we know it, may defeat the goals of our educational enterprise—the development of the individual creativity and autonomy upon which the continuance of our complex, mobile and dynamic society depends. We remain, it is true, fairly naive about the learning that comes from participating in a complex organization versus that which we label mastery of subject matter and for which we test continuously. Is the truant or rebel who evades or rejects the system protesting the controls or the academic requirements of both? Industrial research suggests to us that it is not the task, however difficult or onerous, that contributes to worker malaise—for work can be a challenge or it can be endured—but that it is the sometimes unbearable weight of a supervisory system which restricts the autonomy and creativeness of the individual. This insight should give us pause for in the educational hierarchy, teacher and pupil are at the bottom of the system; they are the recipients, not the originators, of the messages which flow along the line of command. (Kimball, 1963, p. 30).

It also appears to be true that there is little in the environment of many of our schools that stimulates learning by the arousal and rewarding of intellectual curiosity, particularly if it threatens the knowledge of the teacher or what the textbook says. The explosion of knowledge which occurs daily in the modern world and makes textbooks obsolete before they are off the press and teachers uninformed overnight is presenting our schools with a new challenge unlikely to be met by the rigid organizational structure of the past.

THE SOCIAL SETTING OF GUIDANCE

The growth of the school as a bureaucracy has meant an increased arrangement of pupils into categorical groupings. In general these groupings are based on a timetable carefully prepared by curriculum specialists with the aid of child development specialists who have provided American educators with listings of the characteristics of children at each age level. Those children who are on schedule and do the things appropriate to their age are defined as average. Those who are ahead of the schedule are defined as exceptionally gifted and are typically in accelerated classes or even allowed to skip a grade. Those who act younger than their chronological age are categorized as slow and placed in special classes where less is academically required of them or they may be held back and required to repeat a year.

Each school year is culminated by the promotion process in which, if all goes well, a child is advanced into the next grade until the time comes when he is a senior and advanced into the next type of school or out into the world to make a living and establish his own family. In every school, however, there are some children who fail to make the grade and who miss the educational train. Within our slum schools, the proportion of such children is very large. For this reason the slum school offers a particularly unique opportunity to study pupils who are defined as deviant by educators and our society. It also provides a salient spot to observe some of the dilemmas faced by guidance counselors as they work amid educational institutions.

Within the slum school, one cannot but be impressed by the explanations offered for the failure to educate many of the pupils or even to convince them that education is desirable and necessary. An extreme example is provided by the teacher of one second-grade class which the principal describes as wild and other teachers refer to as a zoo and mental institution. This class is one in which physical punishment of the children is frequent and the teacher may be observed pinching the children, twisting their ears, pulling them by the hair or sending them to the corner to stand facing the wall with their hands on their heads. The teacher also occasionally sends for an older student from the fifth grade who forcibly removes children from the room at her request or helps her within the classroom. This boy is regularly assigned to this teacher and on at least one occasion had a fellow classmate as a helper. The removal of the children from the room is described by the teacher as "a method of using one for an example so that the others will behave." She also explains that the children are sent to the principal although a follow-up of this matter by an outsider revealed that the principal never saw the children.

The teacher of the class portrays her seven-year-old children as follows:

> This is a discipline class. It is not an ordinary class. I have emotionally disturbed children and mentally retarded children, and I can't get perfect attention. I don't try to. I can't ride them all the time. . . . The home background of most of the children is simply terrible. All the children are emotionally disturbed. They are really problems. They don't understand normal psychology. They only know brute force. *

Although the class described may be an extreme example of a classroom situation gone awry, the ascription of the difficulty to individual characteristics of the children is common. Scholarly writings and journalistic articles are replete with adjectives describing slum children as unmotivated, culturally deprived, motoric and slow to learn. Without arguing for or against the accuracy of the many adjectives used, it is important that we recognize the function they serve as a rationalization for failure and as a means for categorizing children as non-educable and therefore providing them with nothing but custodial care. Similarly, those who, hearing about such a class, blame it on the personal characteristics of the teacher are also rationalizing failure and removing attention from the system of human relations in which both exist—a system, for example, in which the teacher shortage is so great that it is not unknown for teachers with a bare minimum of training or experience to be hired and having been hired to be assigned to the class with lowest status—i.e., a class in which the children are so far behind in acquiring basic

* This quotation and the descriptions of the second-grade class that precedes it are taken from observational field notes gathered by the author during 1963. Schools observed were public schools located in slum areas of a large Northern city. The second-grade class was comprised of Negro and Puerto Rican children.

skills that they cannot possibly understand the curriculum the teacher has been told to teach.

In the same elementary school as the discipline class, there is a guidance office with a newly arrived energetic full-time guidance counselor. An examination of the records in her office reveals that there are 111 children who are currently in her active file classified into the following categories: acting out, withdrawn, mentally retarded, hyper-active, truants, immature, quiet, rigid, fearful, provocative, day dreamer, temper outbursts, unusual behavior, lack of interest, psychosomatic asthma, slow but not retarded, speech difficulty. Again one notes the tendency to describe children in terms of personal characteristics.

Children who reach the guidance office are frequently accompanied by verbal or written anecdotal records prepared by the teacher who records incidents in which the child has displayed what the teacher perceives to be unusual or non-tolerable behavior. The large number of children enrolled in the slum school and the comparatively small number of guidance counselors often results in a heavy reliance on such records and a consequent bias of the records to a presentation of the child from the teacher's point of view. Even if supplemented by the observations of others, the school records of children both within and outside the guidance office are essentially management's evaluation of child behavior and potentialities. Further, the identification of children as problems within the organization frequently leads to a definition of the child in clinical terms and a concentration on "helping" children to adapt to the organization rather than examining the organization and methods of the school as possible sowers of academic problems (Cicourel & Kitsuse, 1963).

The role of guidance personnel in helping children accept and live within the school organization is well illustrated by the emphasis in guidance lessons taught by teachers who devote part of their time to teaching guidance classes and individual counseling. In one such class, for example, the intellectually-gifted fourth graders are informed that "for a good photograph, we need grooming, washing, dressing, combing and smiling" and that "for a good behavior photograph, we need regular study habits and good manners." Ten junior high school guidance lessons observed by the author in the course of a field study in slum schools were concerned with such topics as participation in extra-curricular activities, dressing well and careers. Even more important as a clue to the role of guidance in the bureaucratic structure is the fact that the guidance curriculum as observed in the above lessons was taught in the same manner as other subjects. The lessons were defined by the teacher and the prescribed course of study. The role of students was that of participating in formal question and answer periods, doing a traditional type of notebook work, or being a committee member on a carefully adult-supervised committee. Only one lesson was observed in which a spontaneous discussion was initiated by pupils. This discussion concerned segregation and occurred when the guidance teacher did not appear, and the students were without a teacher for most of the period.*

Another way in which the work of guidance personnel is affected by the educational bureaucracy results from their position in the administrative hierarchy. As full-time professionals or teachers who have been partially incorporated into the guidance program, the practitioners of guidance are often in a position to initiate action toward other teachers and pupils. For both of these groups, who may already feel that the administration intrudes too often upon their activity, the guidance counselor may only represent one more person who makes unwanted decisions on their behalf. This perception may be heightened by the evaluative judgments guidance counselors make of pupils or teachers, and initial suspicions may be confirmed by the counselor's inability to so change the behavior or placement of difficult pupils that they are no longer a problem for their teachers (Atwood, 1964, pp. 49-77; Cicourel & Kitsuse).

* Twelve lessons were observed in the course of a field study undertaken by the author in slum schools in a large Northern city. All but one of these were in junior high schools. One lesson was in an elementary school.

Anthropologically speaking, guidance may be conceptualized within the theoretical framework provided by empirical studies of socialization. As we have indicated, American schools are formal organizations by means of which the young are prepared for and enter into the adult roles of our society. As American society becomes increasingly complex, one may predict that the bureaucratic socialization process of the modern school will itself become more intricate and that the role of guidance counselors will become increasingly crucial.

Even the cursory observations of guidance programs in slum schools presented in the preceding section are suggestive of the ways in which guidance counselors attempt to facilitate the socialization of slum youngsters so that they may become adapted to school and society. Crucial to the process of socialization is, of course, the selection of children for one of several academic or nonacademic programs within the school. As gatekeepers in the selection process, guidance counselors and their records play a major role although the ramifications of this role are just beginning to be delineated by empirical studies. However, a recent case study of the ways in which an "advanced" suburban high school differentiates students and counsels them toward educational goals provides clues to problems needing further exploration.

Summarizing their findings, Cicourel and Kitsuse report that "our materials indicate a trend towards the rationalization and bureaucratization of the educational system and by implication, of the process of social mobility." The authors continue as follows:

Our case study suggests the emergence of a different form of the ascription or sponsorship principle of placement implemented by a bureaucratic set of procedures. The characteristics that determine placement by this principle would not be the traditional attributes of caste, kinship, race, sex, or other biologically or culturally determined traits of individuals and groups, but the data of test score records, biographical history of family

87

or personal problems, childhood accidents and traumas, academic difficulties, adjustment problems, and the like. The contingencies of social mobility would be controlled within a bureaucratic setting where professional educational doctrines, policies, and practices are fused with clinical and common-sense conceptions to interpret such information and to differentiate the potentially successful from the failures.

The possibility of systematizing the application of this principle of placement is now at hand. Advances in the theory and technology of computer systems provide techniques of processing large numbers of individuals on the basis of standardized units of information. Such units may contain objective as well as subjective information, facts as well as hearsay, rational as well as common-sense interpretations, thus giving due consideration to education not only as a science but also as an art. Insofar as the gathering, coding, and input of such information are bureaucratically controlled, it would be possible to specify the student's probable access to educational opportunities and future life chances by the processing of his cumulative records. In short, the contingencies of social mobility may be rationalized by the use of computer systems in the form of an actuarial table. (Cicourel & Kitsuse, *op. cit.,* pp. 141-42).

When and if the above principles and methods of placement are fully implemented within our educational system, they will have an enormous impact on the socialization of American youth. Even in the limited form in which they are currently found, these principles have produced organizational pressures on schools to identify the academically talented early and to place children in ability groups even in elementary schools so that the intellectually gifted may be free of association with those who are less able. Concomitant strains may be observed among some parents who strive to provide the right experiences for their children from the embryonic stage onward so that their offspring may have at least a fighting chance to be numbered among the bright young children who are on the rise in the educational organization and may eventually wear the child's version of the Brooks Brothers suit complete with attaché case.

Guidance counselors, along with other representatives of management within the school, choose and interpret the tests given to children and write the official biographies of children within the school. Because of this they play a critical role in selecting who will be chosen for which of the several types of socialization offered by the school. Implicit in the selection process is the question of who is to be encouraged and promoted into the professional and managerial roles of society and who is to be relegated to the less rewarding tasks or even abandoned as incapable of any adult work role and suitable only for a dependent role as a welfare client.

In addition to their role in selecting children and youth for the work tasks of the larger society, guidance counselors often must interpret their decisions to these youngsters or others. Psychological interpretations would not appear to be unusual and seem to provide the guidance counselor and other school personnel with a rationalization enabling organizational failures and strains to be minimized or omitted and the nonadaptive characteristics of students or their backgrounds to be heightened. From this point of view the work that guidance performs within the school and the larger society is to "cool out" those who do not fit and to provide reasons for doing so.

ANTHROPOLOGY AND GUIDANCE

In this paper we have stressed the educational environment within which guidance occurs and the relationship of our formal schooling system to American society. Anthropology typically emphasizes the interdependence of the individual and the group or society to which he belongs. It attempts to make explicit the relational system which binds individuals together in the several activities that they share within the several groups of a given society. Although anthropology may classify individuals according to such categorical groups as age, sex, and social status, it seeks the meaning of these categories within the larger society in which they find expression and it then compares one society with another in the pursuit of laws governing human behavior.

To understand guidance, anthropologists would insist that it must be studied within the immediate environment of the schools in which it is found and the larger society to which it is related.

The function of guidance would be analyzed in terms of its interdependence with our educational system and the social system of which both are a part. The counselor-student relationship is of importance to the anthropologist as it is to practitioners and other social scientists, but for the anthropologist the importance of this relationship is to be found within the context of the wider society rather than exclusively within the personality theory of the psychologist or the role theory of the sociologist. In this way anthropology affirms its belief in the organic unity of the individual and his culture.

REFERENCES

Atwood, Mark S. Small-scale administration change: Resistance to the introduction of a high school guidance program. In *Innovation in education,* ed. by Matthew B. Miles. New York: Bureau of Publications, Teachers College, 1964.

Callahan, R. E. *Education and the cult of efficiency.* Chicago: University of Chicago Press, 1962.

Cicourel, A. V. and Kitsuse, J. I. *The educational decision-makers.* New York: Bobbs-Merrill, 1963.

Henry, Jules. *Culture against man.* New York: Random House, 1963.

Kimball, Solon T. and McClellan, James E. *Education and the new America.* New York: Random House, 1962.

Kimball, Solon T. An anthropological view of social system and learning, in *Behavioral Science and guidance,* ed. by Esther Lloyd-Jones and Esther M. Westervelt. New York: Teachers College, 1963.

Mead, Margaret. Our educational emphasis in primitive perspective. *Amer. Jour. of Sociol., 48,* May, 1943.

Poverty and deprivation in the United States. Washington: Conference on Economic Progress, April, 1962.

Spindler, George D. (ed.). *Education and culture.* New York: Holt, Reinhart & Winston, 1963.

ADDITIONAL READING

Benedict, Ruth. *Patterns of culture.* Boston: Houghton Mifflin, 1961.

Boas, F. *Anthropology and modern life.* New York: Norton, 1962.

Chase, S. *The proper study of mankind.* New York: Harper, 1956.

Coleman, J. S. *The adolescent society.* New York: Free Press of Glencoe, 1961.

Ewing, J. F., S.J. Human evolution—1956. In *Anthropological Quarterly*, Oct. 1956, 91-122.

Galdstone, I. *Medicine and anthropology.* Publication of the New York Academy of Medicine, No. XXI. New York: International Universities Press, 1959.

Goldschmidt, W. R. *Exploring the ways of mankind.* New York: Holt, Rinehart & Winston, 1960.

Gruber, F. C. *Anthropology and education.* Philadelphia: Univ. of Pennsylvania Press, 1961.

Haring, D. G. (comp.). *Personal character and cultural milieu.* Syracuse, N.Y.: Syracuse Univ. Press, 1956.

Havighurst, R. *Growing up in River City.* New York: Wiley, 1962.

Honigmann, J. J. *The world of man.* New York: Harper, 1959.

Kardiner, A. *The individual and his society; the psychodynamics of primitive social organization.* New York: Columbia University Press, 1939.

Keesing, F. M. *Cultural anthropology.* New York: Rinehart, 1958.

Kluckholm, C. *Culture and behavior.* New York: Free Press of Glencoe, 1963.

Kluckholm, C. *Mirror for man.* New York: Whittlesey House, 1949.

Kroeber, A. L. *Anthropology: culture patterns and process.* New York: Harcourt, Brace & World, 1963.

Linton, R. *The cultural background of personality.* New York: Appleton-Century, 1945.

Lloyd-Jones, Esther and Westervelt, Esther. *Behavioral science and guidance.* New York: Bureau of Publications, Teachers College, 1963.

Luzbetak, L. J. *The Church and culture.* Techny, Ill.: Divine Word Publications, 1963.

Mead, Margaret. *Childhood in contemporary cultures.* Chicago: Univ. of Chicago Press, 1955.

Mead, Margaret (ed.). *Cultural patterns and technical change.* Paris: UNESCO, 1953.

Mead, Margaret. *Male and Female.* New York: Morrow, 1949.

Mead, Margaret. *The school in American culture.* Cambridge: Harvard Univ. Press, 1951.

Miller, C. H. *Foundations of guidance.* New York: Harper, 1961.

Montagu, A. *Anthropology and human nature.* Boston: P. Sargent, 1957.

Muntsch, A. *Cultural anthropology.* Milwaukee: Bruce, 1934.

Pocock, D. F. *Social anthropology.* New York: Sheed & Ward, 1961.

Redfield, R. *Human nature and the study of society.* Chicago: Univ. of Chicago Press, 1962.

Shapiro, H. L. *Man, culture and society.* New York: Oxford Univ. Press, 1960.

Pauline C. Zischka, Ph.D.

is Chief School Psychiatric Social Worker,
Bureau of Child Guidance, New York City
Board of Education. She received an A.B.
degree at Adelphi University, an M.A. at
Fordham University's School of Social Serv-
ice, and a Ph.D. at New York University.
She is also an assistant professor of guidance
at C. W. Post College. Miss Zischka has had
experience in school social work, supervision
and administration, and her work has in-
volved a great deal of contact with guid-
ance counselors in the field. Her professional
memberships include the National Associa-
tion of Social Workers Council on Social
Work Education. She is a fellow of the Amer-
ican Orthopsychiatric Association and is the
chairman of the By-Laws Committee of that
organization.

Guidance and Social Work

Two allied disciplines, guidance and school social work, have developed side by side in many school systems. These two disciplines may be compared to cousins in the family of the behavioral sciences, who bear a strong resemblance in the eyes of the community and even within the schools. However, they have different talents deriving from important differences in training and techniques. Each profession wants to be known and appreciated for its own contribution. Each is sometimes jealous of its own abilities and a bit fearful of family competition from other behavioral sciences. Together they make one of the most

92

effective teams * now available for dealing with children's problems manifested in the schools.

It is the purpose of this paper to review these two disciplines—guidance and social work—with special emphasis on their shared roots and the areas in which close collaboration is essential if they are to function well together for the greatest benefit of the child, the family and the community.

In considering the relationship between guidance and social work, one might first look carefully at the basic aims of each profession. What do they hope to accomplish? What are their long-range goals? If one were to pose this question to a group of guidance counselors and social workers, the answers would be similar. Both aim toward helping the individual function as a responsible human being, with all of its implications. Both have the purpose of helping the individual to lead a satisfying, effective life, and both recognize that in order to do this, the individual must be helped to realize his fullest potential. Both are cognizant of the need for the individual to be able to function as a responsible member of his society and of society's obligation to make it possible for him to have the dignity and respect to which everyone is entitled. Thus, both guidance and social work are striving toward many of the same common goals.

Next, we should consider the factors that gave the impetus to the development of these two professions. In a general sense, both professions came into being along with a heightened awareness of the fact that while many people can attain their life goals unaided, others, through no fault of their own, need a helping hand. This represented a significant shift from the school of thought which maintained that those who failed, did so because of their own moral weaknesses. For instance, social workers first recognized the fact that contrary to popular legend, few individuals could begin their lives as orphan newsboys and later

* This paper is limited in scope to the relationship of the guidance counselor and social worker, and does not address itself to the more complex settings in which a clinic team, including not only social worker but also psychologist and psychiatrist, are available to work with the counselor and the school.

become heads of corporations. They pointed out that the success of these few did not take away the responsibility of society to do something about the miserable life situations of most of these youngsters. Usually, the conditions of an orphan newsboy's life were so damaging to the individuals involved as to negate the possibility of any type of satisfactory life adjustment. Many of the early social work programs were focused on providing material help to those in need. Various types of institutions were built, including those for orphans, for the aged and handicapped, and there was much emphasis on the giving of alms. As the profession developed, it became clear that providing material help was not the only, or indeed, the best way to meet the needs of these individuals; instead, they needed help in organizing and using their own inner resources. The course of study in preparation for social work then was enlarged to include a focus on the dynamics of human behavior. In addition, as part of the preparation, the social work student had to become aware, through field work and self-examination, of himself and his own motivations, so that these would not be a handicap when he came to help others. Thus, the profession of social work has a dual focus. It is concerned not only with providing the material necessities for an individual to live a satisfying life, but equally, with helping the individual to understand himself and to function at the best level possible for him.

Guidance has also broadened its focus as the profession has developed. Guidance counselors first directed their efforts to providing a kind of informational service about educational and vocational opportunities available to young people. In many ways, this was akin to the social worker's "almsgiving" stage of development. As it became evident that this kind of service did not meet the needs of many of the young people to whom it was given, the counselor's role began to be enlarged. Attention was then directed toward helping the individual students to make the best use of the educational opportunities offered by the schools and the guidance offered by the counselors in the schools. Today, the counselor is keenly aware, for example, of the need to work toward raising the aspirational levels of some of our young people as a prerequisite to providing educational and vocational counseling. Minority group status may tend to discourage aspirations, and in such situations, the counselor must strive to improve the child's self-image and motivate him to greater achievement. In other cases, the counselor may need to focus his attention on work with the parents in order to help them develop more realistic expectations for the child. In each of these instances, the counselor must first arm himself with as complete an understanding of the individual child as is available to him. To do this, he will use a variety of techniques in addition to his own conversations with the child. One of the most significant sources of information about any child is the teacher, for she spends much time with him and observes him in a variety of situations and under a variety of conditions. In addition, the counselor uses the many other sources of information in the school, such as the cumulative record card, medical files, achievement test scores, results of group or individual psychological examinations. In the collection of such data the interest of the two groups comes close together as a social worker who is gathering background information about a child makes use of similar information. He also knows that a teacher's observations are of invaluable aid. He may use them for arriving at a diagnostic formulation concerning a particular child.

There is something else which social workers and guidance counselors both have in common which should serve to bring us closer together. That is the fact that lay people are convinced that they could do both our jobs as well or better than we can. To most people, being a guidance counselor or a social worker appears so simple that they have no doubt that they could start right in without a day's training, but with highly commendable results. Our tools, being in our heads and our personalities, are invisible, and therefore to some may not seem to exist. It behooves us not to make that same mistake about each other.

In the school setting, guidance counselors and social workers occupy the role of specialist, and having this role can pose special problems for both disciplines. Their areas of competence differ from those of the line teaching staff, and this fact in itself can result in their being viewed in a somewhat hostile manner by those who do the actual teaching. Then too, teachers who refer children to the guidance counselor or to the social worker are in the position of asking for help, and this is never an easy thing to do. It may imply a loss of independence or an admission of failure, and there is always the possibility that one's request for help will be refused! Although these feelings may not be recognized consciously by the teacher when she makes the referral, the possibility of their presence cannot be ignored. Further, teachers sometimes view the work of both counselor and social worker as being infinitely easier than that of the teacher, who carries the educational responsibility for a class of some thirty other children in addition to the one who is being referred because of very serious problems. Thus, there is a failure to recognize that the involvement of the guidance counselor with a particular child and that of the social worker with this same child, while differing in many ways, is a demanding one, requiring the highest professional skills each possesses.

PROFESSIONAL TRAINING

Let us turn now to the professional training required for guidance counselors and social workers. A review of the requirements reveals that there are many similarities. Both programs include courses related to psychology, personality development and the basic theories of social and personal behavior. In this sense, both borrow heavily from the other social sciences. Both also include some training in interviewing (although the social worker's training in interviewing formerly was much more intensive; I believe this difference has been eliminated), and both prepare the students for cooperative work with other community agencies and institutions. These similarities in training help in the daily working relationships of the two professions, but they also can lead to problems. Each may secretly believe that he knows as much about the subject as the other, and could do the child considerably more good if he only had the time and opportunity to do so. Such an attitude overlooks the very important differences in training and practice. It is precisely these differences which make for the success of a team approach.

In its simplest terms, the difference between the training of the guidance counselor and that of the social worker is based on the differences in the function of each. The guidance counselor's function is to help all children make the best possible use of the educational opportunities offered to them. This means that he must, himself, intimately understand the teaching process, be able to help teachers as well as students, and must possess a complete knowledge of the various types of curricula, etc. It is for this reason that several years of teaching experience is a prerequisite for guidance counselors. The function of the social worker, on the other hand, is to help people in trouble and his course of study is intensively concentrated on the dynamics of human behavior and the techniques of helping people to organize and use their own inner resources. The social worker understands pathology, and is trained to deal with it. In addition, the social work curriculum attempts to provide an understanding of the effect of social and cultural forces on the adjustment of the individual.

The graduate training program for social workers has two main parts—course work and field work. The field work experience represents a kind of internship for the social work students. With the assistance of the supervisor, the student works with clients in a social agency. Although the number of cases assigned to a student may be smaller than that usually carried by a regular staff member, in other ways he functions as a member of the staff of that agency. Intensive supervision is provided, and the student learns to apply in practice the theory he has been taught in the classroom. His skill in interviewing is developed as he reviews with his supervisor, his handling of each case situation. The student also learns to examine his own motivations, values and needs, so that these will not be a handicap when he comes to help others. In other words, the student develops the skill to be an effective helping person to his clients as the theoretical knowledge is integrated into practice. The importance of the field work experience is evident from the fact that approximately half of the two-year graduate program for social workers is given over to this aspect of training. It is never an elective, but rather, a basic requirement for every social work student. While the focus of a social worker's activity is determined to some extent by the agency setting in which he works, the basic skills are the same regardless of the setting. Thus, a social worker who is part of a school system makes use of the same professional skills and techniques as the social worker who is on the staff of a family service agency. However, each must possess additional knowledge related to the special needs and problems of the clients served.

In order to highlight the relationship between guidance and social work, a description of the activity of the school social worker is necessary. As indicated above, this social worker has completed the prescribed graduate training, and holds the Master of Social Work or Master of Arts degree in social work. He has some knowledge of the school setting, of general educational principles and processes, of curriculum, etc. However, since the roots of his profession are not in the field of education and since he usually does not possess teaching experience, the depth of his understanding in this area is not as great as that of the guidance counselor. When the school social worker and guidance counselor work together, each makes his special contribution. The social worker contributes his skill in understanding the dynamics of the disturbed personality development of a particular youngster. The counselor contributes his knowledge of the teaching process in translating these findings into the best possible kind of educational experience for this child. In those cases in which the social worker carries the responsibility for treatment of the child, the counselor may have little direct contact with the child but, together with the social worker, plays an important role in helping the members of the school staff to understand and accept the child and his educational needs.

In a school setting, the social worker usually has a dual objective. He provides case work help to children and their families, and he provides consultative service to the principal and other school personnel. In serving as a consultant, the social worker assists the school personnel in meeting the educational needs of children who have problems, and assists the principal in arriving at decisions regarding the educational planning for others.

The social worker and guidance counselor must keep in mind the fact that the final responsibility for educational decisions rests with the principal of the school. The principal bears the responsibility for everything that takes place in his school. Further, he must consider the needs of the school as a whole, as contrasted to the needs of a particular student. In order to help children both disciplines must have a good working relationship with the principal. It is not an overstatement to say that the attitude of a principal toward the guidance program in his school is the prime determining factor in the success or failure of that program. If the principal is not convinced of the value of guidance services, he will find it difficult to make the adjustments which make it possible for these services to function most effectively. Such situations tend to be characterized by a paucity of appropriate referrals, by a failure to implement the recommendations made and even by a failure to provide adequate room space for private interviewing.

When a social worker is first assigned to a particular school, his first step is to set up a schedule of regular conferences with the two people with whom he must work most closely—the principal and the guidance counselor. In this way, the social worker learns the needs of the school as the principal sees them, and the principal gains an understanding of the areas in which the social worker can be of greatest assistance to him and his students. Through these conferences, a system for case referral to the social worker is worked out, as well as a method whereby the guidance counselor and the principal are kept informed of developments in the cases already under treatment. As time goes on, the frequency of the principal's attendance at these conferences may be lessened, but he should not delegate all responsibility for the guidance program in the school. To do so might mean that he would lose the help which the guidance counselor and the social worker might provide him in many areas, such as suggestions for curriculum changes, and the need for the establishment of special programs within the school.

The primary source of referral to a school social worker is the guidance counselor. The counselor, in his contacts with teachers, knows which children have given indication of an inability to make a satisfactory school adjustment. He may have suggested a variety of steps to help the child, such as modification of the school program. He may have had contacts with the child and his parents, and from these have obtained a picture of a complex situation. The counselor has usually explored the situation from a variety of viewpoints and has reached the conclusion that the child cannot be helped sufficiently by counseling and other types of educational adjustment. Sometimes, a brief survey of the situation is enough to indicate to the counselor the need for case work involvement. In other situations, a much closer examination of the problem may be necessary. To help the counselor determine which situations should be referred to the social worker, the writer has found the following guidelines to be helpful. Any problems shown by a child, which persist in spite of the best efforts of the school personnel to bring about some improvement, are indicative of the possible need for case work help. Such cases should be referred to the social worker, at least for further diagnostic exploration. The social worker begins by reviewing the information already gathered by the guidance counselor. This usually includes complete information about the child's present and past school adjustment and about his medical record, and he may interview both the child and his parents. Information may also have been received from other agencies to which the child and his family were known. Frequently, the social worker's exploration of the situation merely serves to confirm what the counselor has already ascertained. Nevertheless, there are significant differences in the social worker's approach to a case. These are related to the social worker's training in recognizing and dealing with pathology. In a sense, it might be said that the primary difference between the exploration of a case by a guidance counselor and by a social worker is one of depth. The teacher usually turns first to the guidance counselor for assistance in these situations. By virtue of his special training, the guidance counselor is in a good position to make recommendations for helping the child and to bring the more serious situations to the attention of the social worker. Both of these will be accomplished most effectively if there are regular conferences and close cooperation between the counselor and the social worker.

TYPES OF SERVICES

What are the various types of service provided by the social worker to the children referred to her? These might best be listed briefly as follows:

1. Exploration of the situation from a diagnostic viewpoint, making use of psychological and psychiatric services where indicated.

2. Direct treatment for the child and/or his parents.

3. Referral to the proper community agency for the implementation of recommendations, such as the placement of the child away from his home.

4. Services as a liaison between the school and other community agencies which are active in some of these situations.

5. Consultation with the school personnel about a particular situation.

In addition to these direct services to children, the social worker may also work with groups of teachers or parents. The focus of the social worker's work with teachers is on furthering their understanding of the personality needs of children at certain stages of development, and their understanding of the meaning of deviant behavior. Often, such groups are most effective when they are conducted jointly with the guidance counselor.

The social worker's work with groups of parents may range from a general program of parent education to the conduct of group therapy sessions over an extended period of time. The use of such specialized therapeutic techniques as group therapy or family therapy depends on the skill and experience of the particular social worker in the school. To achieve competence in

101

these areas, the social worker must obtain additional graduate training and experience. As a rule, social workers who have a special interest in doing therapy, devote much of their own time to developing their skills in this area.

The intensity and number of contacts a social worker has in any case depends on the needs of that particular situation. Some situations may require regular weekly contacts with the child and his parents, extending over a period of several months or even years. Others may respond to less intensive treatment, while still others may need only the help provided by the social worker's consultative service.

In summary, there are many areas in which guidance counselors and social workers need to work cooperatively. The social worker who usually has access to psychological and psychiatric services brings to each situation a focus which is essentialy clinical. The special skill of the social worker stems from his training in helping clients to better organize and utilize their own inner resources. He has a deep understanding of the dynamics of human behavior and of the symptoms of pathology. He works intensively with individuals as well as with families, and has to know when and how to use community resources to implement his work. In his relationship with the guidance counselor he is keenly aware of the counselor's knowledge of special resources and techniques which can provide effective liaison between clinical recommendations and educational practice. He looks to the counselor to implement the clinical recommendations in the school setting, and recognizes that this may involve intensive work with teachers which he, lacking the background of an educator, may not be able to do as effectively. Since the social worker is often not present when crises arise in the school adjustment of a youngster with whom he is working intensively, he looks to the guidance counselor to handle these crises. To do this well, the guidance counselor must be aware of the situation. This means that there should be frequent conferences so that the counselor can be kept informed of any changes or developments.

Finally, both professions must be flexible in exploring new

approaches. School guidance teams are pioneers in a relatively new field of applied social science. Out of their work may come not only immediate help to children, but also long-range additions to our incomplete but ever growing knowledge of human behavior.

ADDITIONAL READING

Anderson, J. P. *Opportunities in social work.* New York: Vocational Guidance Manuals, 1957.

Ashdown, Margaret. *Social service and mental health, an essay on psychiatric social workers.* London: Routledge & Paul, 1953.

Biestek, F. P., S.J. *The casework relationship.* Chicago: Loyola, 1957.

Blackey, Eileen. *Group leadership in staff training.* Washington, U.S. Children's Bureau, 1957.

Bogue, D. J. *Skid row in American cities.* Chicago: University of Chicago Press, 1963.

Burchill, G. W. (ed.). *Work study programs for alienated youth.* Chicago: Science Research, 1962.

Clark, K. B. *Prejudice and your child.* Boston: Beacon, 1955.

Conant, J. B. *Slums and suburbs.* New York: McGraw, 1961.

Culbert, J. C. *The visiting teacher at work.* New York: Commonwealth Fund, 1930.

Directory of social and health agencies. New York: Columbia Univ. Press, 1962.

Ferard, Margaret L. *The caseworker's use of relationship.* London: Tavistock, 1962.

Harrington, M. *The other America.* New York: Macmillan, 1962.

Havighurst, R. J. & others. *Growing up in River City.* New York: Wiley, 1962.

Johnson, A. (ed.). *School social work.* New York: National Assoc. of Social Workers, 1962.

Kahn, A. J. *Planning community services for children in trouble.* New York: Columbia Univ. Press, 1963.

Lichter, S. O. & others. *The dropouts.* New York: Free Press of Glencoe, 1962.

Myrdal, G. *An American dilemma.* New York: Harper, 1944.

National Conference on Social Welfare. *Social work practice.* New York: Columbia U. Press, 1962.

Passow, A. H. (ed.). *Education in depressed areas.* New York: Columbia Univ. Press, 1963.

Polansky, N. A. *Social work research.* Chicago: Univ. of Chicago Press, 1960.

103

Riessman, F. *The culturally deprived child.* New York: Harper, 1962.

Roth, N. R. *Reaching the hard to reach.* New York: Huntington Family Center, 1961.

Sexton, Patricia C. *Education and income.* New York: Viking, 1961.

Sorokin, P. A. *Altruistic love.* Boston: Beacon Press, 1950.

Voiland, Alice L. & associates. *Family casework diagnosis.* New York: Columbia Univ. Press, 1962.

Where to find vocational training in New York City. New York: Vocational Advisory Service, 1962.

Woodfork, N. C. *Social work techniques utilized in the treatment of psychotic patients.* Amherst, Mass.: Woodfork & Hayes, 1957.

Periodicals

Social Service Review
Social Service Yearbook
Social Work Journal

James M. Somerville, S.J.

*is Associate Professor and Chairman of the
Department of Philosophy of Fordham University. His B.A., M.A., and Ph.D. were
awarded at Fordham University. At Oxford
and the Sorbonne he pursued post-doctoral
studies in philosophy. He is a member of
the following professional associations: the
Realist Society, the American Philosophical
Association, the Metaphysical Society, and
the American Catholic Philosophical Association of which he is a member of the executive committee. His journal articles in
professional publications include: "The Theory and Practice of Action," "Language as
Symbolic Function," "Maurice Blondel:
1861-1961." He also wrote the foreword and
contributed a chapter to* A Modern Introduction to Metaphysics *(ed. D. A. Drennen).
Since 1961 he has been executive editor of
the* International Philosophical Quarterly.

Philosophy, Guidance, and Freedom

It is impossible to help people to help themselves if they do
not believe that they are free. The counselor and the counselee
work together to learn the counselee's past motivation and to
deepen and broaden his range of choices, in the hope that he
will freely and spontaneously do what is for his own best interests. From one point of view, then, guidance may be defined
as the art of helping people realize that they are free and that
they need not be victims of circumstances, impulses, blind drives,
and compulsions.

Perhaps it strikes you as strange that we should be speaking
of the importance of showing people that they are free. Do we

not witness today the spectacle of too much freedom? Is not the current epidemic of lawlessness a proof that freedom has gone too far and that we are in need, not of more but of less freedom? To begin with, "freedom" is an ambiguous word. If by freedom you mean a lack of physical restraint, then, of course, a tiger in the jungle is free. So also is a criminal at large free—or for that matter anyone who is not in jail. And I suppose you could say, in this perspective, that those who flaunt the law and get away with it are free, at least free from the sanctions of the law. But freedom in all these instances is simply immunity from external coercion or restraint, and it has very little in common with that deeper freedom of the spirit which neither beasts nor criminals can understand because they are ruled by appetite, instinct, and passion. The lawless man is not master in his own house, and therefore he is not really free.

And this may be the reason why, in spite of all the talk about freedom in our day, many of our younger people seem to be less and less convinced that they are free. Since we live in a relatively affluent culture, where even the advertisements appeal to the most primitive appetites and instinct, and where everything suggests comfort, ease, and obedience to the laws of hedonism, it becomes increasingly difficult for the ordinary citizen to experience that sense of freedom that comes when a man exercises conscious dominion over his appetites. When the pressures that militate against freedom and self-determination are so strong, is it so surprising that teenagers try to vindicate their freedom by doing odd and offbeat things, what I might call "groundless" actions that seem to have no rhyme or reason? And that is precisely the point: these actions are unpredictable and unforeseen, even by the actors themselves. Nothing is planned or determined. Everything is gung-ho, caprice, and quite mad. You "flip" like an animated pancake, and nobody knows what is coming next.

It is not so much a question of being anti-social nor of enjoying the reputation of being an outlaw. The important thing is to prove that, unlike the commonality of men, you are not determined by custom or law, nor even by common sense and reason. What is predictable is predetermined and necessary;

what comes off the top of the head, like a wanton act of vandal-
ism or a senseless assault on another person, is ideally suited
to demonstrate one's freedom. Surely, one of the major obstacles
to success in guidance is the hidden and often unconscious conviction of so many young people that they are not really free,
or that freedom is only vindicated by some kind of outrageously
offbeat or groundless action.

I wish to analyse some of the factors that have contributed to
the illusion of determinism or, if you will, to the mute and un-
spoken belief that we are so governed by inner and outer forces
that the area of freedom has shrunk to the vanishing point. In
more sophisticated circles there is a tendency to equate freedom
with our ignorance of motives and causes. In this view a free
act is one that we cannot *now* explain, though obviously it
must be motivated—and therefore determined—by factors which,
if known, would reveal that it was merely the product of neces-
sitating causes and conditions. Thus there is a striking parallel-
ism between the views of certain academicians and many young
people who are in need of guidance. And they are in need of
guidance precisely because they unconsciously hold a philosophical view about freedom which reduces it to the realm of the ir-
rational. Or to put it the other way: it is thought that once
you understand the motives and reason which condition an
action, that is, once it is seen to be a rational consequence of
intelligible antecedents, then it is no longer free. And therefore
the only area left to freedom is that which is concerned with
the unintelligible, the groundless, and the absurd. For purposes
of guidance, I think that it is very important for all of us to
understand the very close relationship between classical philosophical positions on freedom and the hidden convictions that
are reflected in the attitudes of the girl or boy on the street.

THE DETERMINISM OF INNER AND OUTER PRESSURES

Let us begin with some of the very obvious outer pressures
that tend to limit a person's power of self-determination. Clearly,
when a man is in jail he is not at liberty; he is restrained by

107

outer forces which take the form of walls, guards, and iron bars. But there is another type of outer force which acts in function of man's psychological nature and attitudes. In this case the force that determines or limits our exercise of freedom is more social than material.

To take an example: social analysts and psychologists, not to mention writers of popular books on behavior, are fond of stressing the role of conformism, that is, the tendency on the part of the individual to make the criterion of his action the opinion of his companions or the society in which he lives. He is, in a word, "outer directed." Such a person easily becomes a victim of propaganda, since he has few internal resources which could enable him to resist any strong current of ideas, especially when presented after the manner of the hard sell and repeated over a considerable period of time. He is highly suggestible, almost protoplasmic in his ability to drift with the tide.

Depersonalized Authority. Allen Wheelis in *The Quest for Identity* points out that modern psychiatry is greatly concerned with the shift in the normative for human action from the father image of the Victorian period and before (the "stern old man who gives the law") to the group image (pp. 126ff.). In the latter case the individual seeks security in conforming to what the multitude approves. This is not really so new, of course: human respect has always been an important factor in influencing behavior. But what is new is the decline in the role of the person in the moral sphere. This is due, in part, to the rise of democracy and government by law rather than by the will of the monarch or ruler. But Immanuel Kant has also had something to do with it. In his moral philosophy Kant stressed the notion of duty for duty's sake. We do not obey the law for the sake of another person nor to please any one, but we obey because obedience is a good which needs no justification (pp. 393-405).

This depersonalization of the motive for moral conduct was, no doubt, one of the earliest and no doubt necessary attempts to demythologize ethics. Kant did not want the ground for any moral action to be anthropomorphic, and in order to purify the moral response it had to flow from an interior categorical imperative that was in no sense the voice of another person, even though it commanded us to respect persons. In this sense Kant, whether for better or worse, was far ahead of his time. Morality today, especially public morality, is largely an impersonal matter. We obey laws, not persons. As a consequence we have very little sense of responsibility—and I use the word responsibility here in its etymological sense: our obedience to the law is not really a *response* such as would exist in a dialogue between one person and another. I may be a person, but the law is not. Therefore, I cannot enter into any kind of communion with it. The law is cold and abstract, and if I "obey" it, even the term obedience has a quasi-mythic quality about it. The law is not a person, and therefore strictly speaking I cannot obey it; I can only submit to its stipulations. But that makes it a bit like playing a game according to the rules, and if you do not like the rules you can always make up your own. In other words, once law becomes disassociated from the person of the lawgiver, it is no longer a subject for reverence and respect. It has lost its authority: *auctoritas.* Just as responsibility implies a dialogue between persons, and just as obedience includes the notion of a response to the will of another person, in like manner we attribute authority to persons and obey the person who has authority.

But to obey for duty's sake and not for the sake of another takes responsibility out of the interpersonal context. And this is what has happened in our teeming democracies. The laws and the source of law have become so depersonalized and demythologized that they have lost their humanity, that is, their status as a manifestation of the personal wish and good pleasure of a personal ruler. If today, then, there is a lot of resistance to the idea of authority, it is partly due to the fact that the younger generation feels differently about the nature of law than the generations that preceded it. The law is no longer viewed as coming from the Wise Old Man who is the repository of all authority. It is simply an impersonal code, which is more frequently an obstacle to the fulfillment of one's personal ambitions.

So it easily becomes the enemy, or if that is too anthropomorphic, it becomes a burden and an inconvenience.

Why, then, should one submit to the prescriptions of any law? Certainly not because law enjoys any "authority" of its own; certainly not because it expresses the personal will of a respected lawgiver. And as for performing one's duty for duty's sake, this is like attributing the sweetness of sugar to its sacchrine flavor. It explains nothing. But if the law has lost its authority because the person behind the law has been lost to view, are we not better off? It would seem to be quite in line with the ideals of Western democracies to favor government by law rather than by personalities. It gives greater stability to institutions, as we saw at the time of President Kennedy's death, when the Ship of State managed to sail on quite smoothly in spite of the change of command. We are no longer at the mercy of the patriarchal type of government where the happiness of the people is almost entirely dependent upon the character of the ruler. What has happened in government has also happened in big business, big education, and big guidance. A constitutional type of procedure has replaced the older personal relationship between ruler and subject, craftsman and apprentice, patron and worker. One obvious effect of this is that people no longer have a feudal sense of loyalty to those in authority. For whether one is dealing with the family, the corporation, the school, the government, or even the Church, when the exercise of authority has not become odious it has become almost completely anonymous. If, at one time, men obeyed in order to please their father, or patron, or monarch, there is no such incentive today. There is a penalty for incorrect behavior and certain rewards for doing things "the company way," but virtue, so defined, is hardly the result of loyalty or devotion to any mythical or real person. What one pleases is a faceless and anonymous un-person, the company or the group. For youth this becomes the clique, the crowd or the gang.

The quest for one's personal identity is one of the principal concerns of man in the second half of the twentieth century. Who am I? What function do I fulfill in society? In a culture

110

where the norms for acceptable behavior were somewhat more closely attached to the approval of the one in authority, it was easier to discover one's own identity. But once the criterion for moral action becomes the approval of the group or a mere climate of opinion, it is difficult for a person, especially a young person, to discover anything like a moral absolute. Everything dissolves and is carried away in the flux of opinion. For pragmatic social norms change with each generation and hardly provide an unfailing and unchanging ethical North Star. The very mutability and impersonality of public opinion is disconcerting for one who has an urge to commit himself to a law that is rooted in the will of an infinite Person. And in one way or another, we all have this desire and need to ground law in the person and in the absolute.

Conformism. I do not think that the revolt against authority should be construed as a rebellion against the absolute. It is precisely because man needs a personal absolute that he goes adrift when he is asked to make an impersonal relative the norm and criterion for his conduct. When the Bohemian or the beatnik seeks to recover a sense of his own identity by challenging the mores of an artificial society, his attack on bourgeois conformism is an attempt to reaffirm the sacredness of the individual and the person against the leveling and impersonal pressures of public opinion. It may be, of course, that this too is a kind of conformism, since the esoteric circle of non-conformists constitutes an upside down group of people who seek to be different by becoming alike—not unlike those women who have a passion to adopt the latest styles so that they may distinguish themselves by becoming exactly like everyone else in the avant-garde group. There is in all of this the sense of being outer-directed, with the corresponding loss of internal initiative and freedom.

And this brings us back to the original point, namely, that among the factors that limit our exercise of freedom, or at least give us the illusion that we are not free, are to be numbered the external pressures that tend to make us conform to what the group approves, without any reference to a person or to an absolute.

111

Advertising and Sincerity. In this connection many studies have been made of advertising and propaganda both in the political and commercial areas. Some vague knowledge of the methods of Nazism and Communism, coupled with a distaste for the hard sell, have made people wary of pitchmen, whether they are retailing snake oil, bufferin, or old-time religion. We know that we are largely victimized by the bunk and ballyhoo of our communications services. Those with a little experience rarely believe everything they read in the newspapers because they do not believe that reporting and newscasting are objective or even accurate. No doubt scepticism in these matters can be excessive, but the public is becoming more circumspect; so true is this that it is hard to get people to commit themselves to anything. Many young people have come to the point where they do not believe anything they are told. Moreover, they suspect even the saint and the social worker of having ulterior motives. They are so alert to this overriding prevalence of self-interest that they are apt to regard it as *the* determining factor in all human action and aspiration. If this were the case, as the utilitarians of all ages have always maintained, then there would be very little room left for freedom since man would always be determined by what appeared to him to be the greatest good in terms of his personal interests. Yet so convinced are some people of the insincerity of everyone else that insincerity, taken for granted, has been made the theme of one of the year's most successful Broadway plays. We have been moved from "How to Win Friends and Influence People," to "How to Succeed in Business— by Being Totally Insincere." People can laugh at this only because they are forced to recognize that much of it is all too true. Authenticity is not only not a virtue; some regard is as not even possible. Thus, the whole world has become phony, as the youthful hero in Salinger's book complained when, like Diogenes, he took his lantern and set out in search of an honest man (1945).

If it is true, then, that we do take our norms from the group and that even those who protest against conformity only do so in order to acquire status, it looks as though one is damned if one conforms and damned if one does not. And there are some

112

who would be quite willing to leave it at this. On such terms
sincerity becomes impossible, because no matter what you do you
are always being motivated by selfishness and self-interest. "Nobody ever does anything except for selfish reasons," says the
popular comedian, Jerry Lewis, as reported in a recent issue of
the *Saturday Evening Post* (p. 86) . "I understand that," he continues, "because someone else is benefitting from what I do
doesn't make what I've done less selfish. It doesn't make it as
bad, that's all." So Mr. Lewis, after having given away some six
million dollars to various charities, insists that it was all done
for kicks. Of course, it is a rather harmless way of being selfish,
an enlightened form of self-interest, the innocent pastime of a
man who likes to play Maecenas, and I suspect that Mr. Lewis is
more authentically generous than he is willing to admit. But
what is interesting is his own evaluation of himself and, I suppose, of Everyman. It is so symptomatic of our times: virtue is
vice, altruism is selfishness, and anyone who pretends to act
with pure motives is by that fact deceiving himself. All that we
have done is to sophisticate the law of the jungle by making it
less harmful.

So when you get a crazy mixed-up kid who comes to you with
his problems, he probably has a sneaking suspicion that he is
playing out a little game, that you the test giver or head shrinker,
or whatever you think you are, are playing yours; that your pre-
tended interest in him is part of the game; that you get something
out of it, whether you realize it or not. And when all is said and
done this complicated young person may feel infinitely superior
to you because he, at least, knows that human nature is a fraud,
whereas you are naive enough to believe that sincerity is possible. Thus, a bit of Freud has seeped down to the masses: the
forces that determine us to act are occult and concealed in the
unconscious. We are driven on by secret wish-fulfilling desires
and complexes. As a consequence the idea that there could be
such a thing as spontaneous goodness is something out of Hans
Christian Andersen. Nobody is free from the determinism of self-
interest. In fact, freedom is just as much an illusion as generosity,
detachment or spontaneous goodness.

FREEDOM AND PHILOSOPHY

Twenty-five years ago students used to argue abstractly over the freedom of the will, and a favorite canard in those days was the notion that you are always determined by the weightier motive. When you choose the smaller piece of pie in order to prove that you are free and not determined by self-interest, you are in fact determined by the greater and more advantageous motive. For at the moment it is more to your advantage and self-interest to choose the lesser good since it will help you to prove your point. So you are always determined by self-interest and there is no such thing as freedom. All of that was academic and good fun in a campus bull session. But today it is no longer merely academic. Neither has Kant, nor Freud, nor Dewey remained in the classroom. The cynicism of youth is partially based on this very supposition that there is no such thing as genuine detachment, because you are always determined by some secret motive that smacks of self-interest. Of course, it is easy to see this in someone else, but what is curious about the present trend in the literature of confession or self-revelation is that it tends to be so self-depreciating. So we get involved in the highly complex situation of having to deal with people who, in order to reassure themselves about their own sincerity, write at length and in public about how insincere they are. This is the sophistication of sophistication and when you have to deal with a young person whose mind works this way, you have your hands full.

Thus far, we have spoken of exterior and interior pressures that create the illusion of determinism. Kant was the most venerable of the philosophers referred to. But if we cared to push the matter, we could trace the history of the determinism of self-interest to the Greek Sophist, Gorgias, or to the Roman Hedonist, Lucretius. A much more sophisticated version, however, can be found in Spinoza, and while he died almost three hundred years ago, it is amazing how the contemporary view of freedom (or the lack of it) harkens back, not to the Sophists or Epicureans but to Spinoza.

114

PHILOSOPHY, GUIDANCE, AND FREEDOM

Spinoza. Spinoza was a rationalist. Now the chief aim of rationalism was to reduce the whole of reality to a system of intelligible principles from which one could deduce a set of certain consequences. As Stuart Hampshire remarks, "Spinoza does not, and cannot, distinguish between the 'cause of an idea' and the 'logical ground' of an idea" (p. 125). This means that Spinoza did away with efficient causality. A certain state (B) is not produced or caused by a state (A), but is a logical deduction from it. The logic of rationalism is a formalistic logic, and just as conclusions in logic derive necessarily from their antecedents, so in human action (where the will is no longer the efficient cause of action), every act follows necessarily and with ineluctable logic from the complexus of its antecedents. Therefore, if you know all of the antecedents, it is easy to deduce the consequent. What Spinoza is saying is that every event, even so-called free actions, are determined by antecedent factors. In spite of this radical determinism, Spinoza does not find that it contradicts his definition of freedom. For Spinoza a man is most free when he knows clearly all the conditions and antecedents of an act. In a word: freedom is adequate knowledge. Servitude is the result of inadequate knowledge or ignorance. Now a person who has adequate knowledge will see that the freest act is the one that is deducible with logical necessity from its antecedents or ground. Paradoxically, then, a man becomes free only when he understands that all is necessary. This is undoubtedly a strange notion of freedom, since it comes down to saying that a man is free when he sees clearly that he is not free. But let us not be too hasty in blaming the philosopher for uttering nonsense. Spinoza's view does not differ very much from notions you can pick up on the sidewalks of New York. Putting aside, for a moment, Spinoza's curious use of the term "freedom," what he is saying is that every event or action, whether we realize it or not, is completely determined; it is the necessary and logical consequence of a set of antecedent conditions. When a man does not understand all these conditions, or when he supposes that he is the real, efficient cause of his own free actions, then he is ignorant or deceived. He has confused freedom with ignorance of the determining conditions. On the other hand, when a man does understand all of the conditions which determine his act, then he is free. Freedom, therefore, is the understanding of necessity. Or to put it another way: freedom is understanding. Throughout the *Ethics,* Spinoza never for a moment surrenders the rationalistic presupposition which denies freedom to the will (even denying that there is a will), and redefines freedom in terms of the intellect. But if everything is determined, there is no such thing as choice. Everything that we do is the result or consequence of exterior and interior pressures and conditions. But isn't this exactly the same notion that we have already described in its popular manifestations? The young man who believes that all is determined by self-interest, that those who think they are generous or altruistic are deceived; the one who believes that Freudian compulsions and complexes rule our actions and that when you dig a little into the unconscious you will find that instincts, impulses, and blind drives are the real "causes" of free acts; those who attribute the illusion of freedom to our ignorance of hidden motives: are they not subscribing to the central Spinozan position which assumes that all is determined and necessary and freedom can only be saved by changing its definition?

Hegel, Marx, and Dewey. If we jump forward some 150 years to Hegel, we find a theme that is not unlike that of Spinoza, except that Hegel who died in 1831 has translated Spinoza's static determinism into a dynamic and moving dialectic. Unlike Spinoza, Hegel was interested in history and society, and his logic is not an abstract deductive one—at least in the Phenomenology—but a logic of the concrete (Collins, 1954, Ch. 14). This means that for Hegel any given moment in history is the logical outcome of all that has gone before. Each trend begets its opposite, and the synthesis of opposites produces a new moment, which has grown out of the past. Therefore, society at any given period or place is the latest fruit of the historical antecedents of the race. As for the individual, each person is a focal point in the whole complexus of society and history, and his being and meaning can only be defined in terms of the whole

116

historical and social process. Process is history; context is society. Put them together and you have Hegel's concrete logic which, in a most remarkable way, seeks to reduce the contingencies of time and place to moments in the dialectic whereby Absolute Spirit manifests Itself in history. Thus, in the evolving web of circumstances, every individual (and especially the great philosophers) become necessary moments in the great movement through which Absolute Spirit utters itself, acquires content, and returns to its source.

Perhaps you are wondering at this point what these cosmic considerations of Hegel have to do with guidance. Well, first of all, Communism is one of the by-products of Hegelianism, although Hegel himself would hardly have subscribed to the philosophy and economics of Karl Marx. What Marx did was to provide a materialistic interpretation of Hegel's dialectic of history. Like Hegel, Marx maintained that society at any given given moment is the fruit of its historical antecedents. But unlike Hegel, who did not like to predict the future but only to interpret the past, Marx insisted that history was moving necessarily toward the overthrow of capitalism and individualism, and that a classless society would eventually arise out of the ashes of the proletarian revolution. The role of the Communist party is to hasten the inevitable revolution. The individual acquires his meaning, not as an isolated atom, but in society and in the community. He is a contextual being who, if he fails to cooperate with the forces of evolution in its necessary movement toward the eschatological moment of total Communism, must be eliminated.

Now in order to make sure that each individual does move with the inevitable historical process, Marxism makes a maximal use of propaganda, the hard sell, high pressure methods—along with a few thumb screws or the equivalent—to induce the proper progressive attitudes. Communists, then, to the extent that they are determinists, believe that it is quite possible to create a new kind of man by propaganda and selective education. Man's freedom, if it exists, will be found in his ready acceptance of the inevitable victory of the Revolution and in cooperation with

117

the aims of the Party. So we are back again with Spinoza and his definition of freedom, viewed as the understanding of what is necessary, determined, and inevitable.

Back of the Communist program, then, is the familiar notion that the thinking habits and attitudes of men can be induced and manipulated at will by exerting inner and outer pressures. Under the barrage of intensive propaganda, no man can stand up. If he tries to, then he must be eliminated, regretfully but with forcefulness and courageous determination. Thus, not only is man the necessary product of evolution, not only is history a necessary process leading to Communism, but man's freedom is so conditioned by social and psychological factors that even his thoughts and attitudes can be manufactured so that men think what the Party wants them to think.

In the United States, we are, of course, greatly revolted by Communism, and our attachment to freedom would seem to make us the polar opposite of Marxist thinking. But there are curious affinities. It is certainly no accident that, for all practical purposes, contemporary American philosophy began with the Hegelian movement and *The Journal of Speculative Philosophy*. Interest in Hegel continued throughout the lifetime of *The Journal*, and James, Dewey, and Josiah Royce all had strong Hegelian leanings, at least at the start. Obviously, the American interpretation of Hegel was not the same as that of Karl Marx. The expanding frontier and the belief in America's limitless opportunity modified the Neo-Hegelian dialectic of history, eliminating some, but by no means all, of the historical determinism. "Manifest Destiny" played its part in American thinking as well as in Marxist expansionism. But in this country Hegel was less important politically than socially. For the social philosophy of John Dewey is inexplicable without Hegel. Dewey, of course, is much more careful to stress the importance of freedom and the individual's initiative, but he still sees the individual largely as the product of social forces. Technological and economic factors shape our thinking and attitudes by producing new needs which stimulate new inventions. And these in turn create changing moral views. In the dialectic between man and

118

his environment (which for Dewey includes nature and technology), it is the environment which plays a preponderant role in creating the New Man of secularist humanism. Having been gradually emancipated from the influence of institutions, Humanity, in Dewey's view, is now borne along and molded by social and environmental factors. Rapid communication, the press, household conveniences, and the schoolroom are the dominant elements which produce and form the New Man. Everything, then, is in a state of flux, and the morality of any generation develops largely in function of the social forces that are at work at any given moment.

Dewey's philosophy is remarkable free from the I-Thou concerns that seem to plague the Existentialists. He is certainly interested in the self-realization of the person, but the person is more often viewed as an individual in society. And if one had to characterize his thought as standing somewhere between rugged individualism and cultural socialism, there can be no doubt about where we would have to situate him. Dewey's sense of community and of the importance of external factors in molding the individual are dominant in his thought, so much so that the individual seems at times to be nothing more than the point of intersection of a complex of forces and pressures. Thus, one of the by-products of the environmental school's insistence on the influence and action of circumstantial factors in creating new attitudes is the growing popular belief that man is the necessary product of his environment and that there is very little room for freedom.

When this popularization joins hands with the Freudian notion that we are also determined by unconscious inner drives, we are greeted by a generation that mistrusts itself and its own motives and suspects that everyone is like so much flotsam and jetsam, tossed about by mysterious inner and outer forces, all of which greatly curtail the horizon of freedom. Each individual is little more than a point of convergence for environmental and unconscious influences. The contemporary mood of psychological realism among youth has little place for altruism and detachment. It is an outlook that is cynical and radically sceptical about

119

the whole enterprise: "Nice guys finish last," and they get what they deserve. The only way to get ahead is to develop a tough hide, admit that everyone is a fraud, oneself included, and forget about trying to make this world a better place to live in. When we pretend that we are unselfish, generous, noble, or free from the determinism of self-interest, we are greatly deceived.

GROUNDS FOR OPTIMISM

I do not pretend that these attitudes are universal, nor do I hold that all of them can be traced to well-defined philosophical positions. But philosophical ideas do have consequences. In time they find expression in popular attitudes. Perhaps all of this represents America's coming of age. At least we are no longer naïve. The questioning attitude is not in itself bad or vicious. It enables one to avoid being a dupe, and it tends to be intolerant of intolerance, as though anyone had an exclusive monopoly on truth—whatever that is. In other words, while the older generation professes that it is greatly puzzled by youth's cynicism, I think that there is a good side to this. If youth no longer accepts anything "as advertised" and at its face value, it is because it wants reasons. If you make a law and want it to be obeyed, it behooves you to supply satisfactory reasons for making the law in the first place. If a ruling or regulation seems to be arbitrary, archaic, or unnecessary, there will be trouble. But once you can justify your order, the rebellion usually ceases. This may be wearisome for oldsters whose idea of efficiency does not leave time for long explanations, but we are long past the day when we can dispense with them. And this was the point of Andrew M. Greeley's article in *America* about "The New Breed" (1964, pp. 706-09). The very students who will plague the administration of a college about the way the place is run, require that its president justify his existence and regulations, lead sit-ins and anti-authoritarian riots, are frequently the ones who will join the Peace Corps, teach catechism in the slums, and try in other ways to justify their existence.

Youth's Attachment to Authenticity. Contemporary youth is not incapable of rising to a high ideal, but it wants to know all the angles so that it can do away with cant and the cult of the phony, especially by those in positions of responsibility. In the midst of all the muddle and the belief in the determinism of inner and outer forces, there is something terribly pure and earnest at the core. It betrays, I think, a fierce attachment to truth. And here psychology bears us out; for is it not true that those who seem to be obsessed with the notion that all is humbug are, in fact, passionately devoted to authenticity?

We began by suggesting that one of the functions of guidance is to help people realize that they are free, for unless a person believes that he is free he will not be able to help himself. Assuming that the diagnosis is correct, what remedy can the philosopher offer? The only way you can convince anyone that freedom exists is to have him experience it. There is no sense in trying to argue about it, for as Henri Bergson has pointed out, every attempt to demonstrate freedom plays into the hands of the determinists. The only proof of the pudding in this case is in the eating. When a man has performed a free action and has experienced its liberating power, then the moral life has begun.

The first step is to get a person to perform a completely unselfish action. And in this endeavor I do not find that the traditional scholastic approach in ethics is adequate, at least as a pedagogical instrument. Here the moral life is usually presented as involving a choice between good or bad actions. The end is eternal beatitude and a good action is represented as a means for attaining this end. An action is said to be good when it is in harmony with the exigencies of rational human nature. When one's whole life is so ordered, beatitude follows as a natural reward. For the modern student the whole approach is too abstract, too self-centered, too much given to stressing the importance of individual happiness as a *quid pro quo* for good behavior. If you want to be happy, behave. It sounds suspiciously like the old enlightened self-interest of Mill and the utilitarian school. So it turns out that morality is a deal! People go in for it because they expect a kickback or reward! Once again the determinism of self-interest raises its ugly head.

The Response to Value. But what about a really unselfish action? One that would be completely undetermined by any mercenary motives? Whether or not philosophy, by itself, is capable of providing grounds for such an ideal, it is certain that the Gospel has provided it. I do not think that you have to prove that the Good Samaritan did the right thing. Who can doubt that mercy and compassion are values that need no defense? What is interesting in this parable is the fact that nowhere does our Lord say that the Samaritan received or sought a reward. He simply did what was right without stopping to consider whether or not there was anything in it for him. The universal brotherhood of man is something that most people can understand, and unless one has been corrupted by prejudice or some form of parochialism, it is not necessary to try to justify interracial justice or neighborly conduct. What is good is good. The important thing is to respond generously to objective values, not letting the left hand know what the right is doing. Then we can forget about selfish motives. Perhaps we may on occasion catch ourselves in the act of washing the outside of the cup, wearing our fringes long, or carrying our phylacteries prominently. Then learn the lesson. Next time, perform your action in secret, make sure that the one you help cannot return the favor, and above all do not think about what you have done, lest you have your reward in the complacency that follows. And then when you have done all that you should do, be sure to remind yourself that you are still an unprofitable servant.

This philosophy, which is not preached enough, constitutes the real revolution, and it is the only thing left that can appeal to a generation that is in danger of losing its faith in human nature and freedom. Christianity is still the great challenge to the contemporary dogma of psychological determinism and the belief that there is no such thing as true detachment. It is only by performing truly generous actions that promise no gain for oneself that man's freedom can be demonstrated, because in this case alone is one responding to an objective need of another and not merely fulfilling a subjective satisfaction. One who performs a good and charitable action simply because it is good and for no other "reason" escapes the network of inner and outer forces and determinisms which, under analysis, recede into conditions conditioning conditions, ad infinitum. It is in this kind of challenge that a man discovers that he is free, and with a single "I will," *sic volo*, he can confiscate all the subaltern determinisms and use their psychic energy and dynamism in order to focus it all in a unitary way on a single object or work that has a value in itself. Do not ask what profit your action will have for yourself, but ask what you can do to profit someone else. This is the light that can truly light the world. And the world of youth is ready for it.

Youth is tired of all that is inauthentic and phony, tired of being told that it is not free because it is determined by environment and hidden motivation. If a young man once understands the meaning of this declaration of independence that is Christianity, if he can see or be shown that a truly generous act and a dedicated life are the proof that man is free; then we have refuted rationalism, utilitarianism, and all of the other forms of determinism which implicitly or explicitly deny the possibility of a truly disinterested goodness and of an action that is a response to an objective value rather than to a subjective need or satisfaction.

The real test of freedom is when one does what is good simply because it is good, not just because it is in harmony with man's rational nature in all its aspects, nor because it is a means to happiness. It can be all of these but in one sense the freest act is the act that is unconditioned and, in one sense, "unmotivated." What do I mean by saying that in one sense the free act is unmotivated? Is this not equivalent to reducing freedom to a form of irrationalism? No, what I have tried to do is to state the case in a dramatic and almost shocking manner in order to highlight the contrast between psychological or subjective determinism and the objective value response. In responding to an objective situation which may make great demands on my generosity I am not acting without a motive or a reason. The motive for my action is the need of another. But in this ideally generous act I do not look to myself nor to my own advantage. I have no subjectively satisfying motive, or at least it is certainly not the determining one. There is nothing subjectively satisfying about being crucified or laying one's life down for another. There is a motive, in the objective order, and it is concerned with the supreme value of the human person, but there is nothing in it for me. If you risk your life to save another man from drowning, you do not do it because of self-interst. You do it because of the objective value of a human life. And it is this kind of act that I say is unmotivated; unmotivated, that is, according to any subjectively satisfying consideration.

In the guidance of youth it seems to me to be of supreme importance today to present the young with this ideal of total dedication and to challenge them to try to act without thought of self. This is quite revolutionary; in fact, it is the gospel which Christ Himself announced and exemplified. St. Paul called it the power of God, but it is also the road to freedom. Why? Because it forces the individual to look away from himself and to lose himself in a life of dedication to others.

Authenticity and the Counselor. It all seems so obvious, but it is not an easy lesson to teach unless the counselor himself is committed to it. He must be more than an employee of an agency, more than a functionary doing a job for a salary. One can talk, advise, analyse, and prescribe for months on end and get nowhere because one is very often playing into the trap of psychological determinism by seeking reasons for reasons and conditions for conditions, again ad infinitum. But the counselor must learn to cut through all of this by his own attitude of generosity and profound love. In the end this is the only thing that persuades; for the person you are trying to help must be able to see in you the very thing that you are trying to make him see. Will you withdraw because of the fear of being hurt by ingratitude? Will you complain because in many cases you fail to reap any personal satisfaction? If this is the case, then it is probable that you, yourself, are unconsciously playing the angles. You want something back for your trouble.

124

But suppose, instead, you simply do what has to be done, not looking to the left or the right, not caring whether you receive kicks or thanks, not looking for that hidden bonus. Suppose you set aboout doing what is good simply because it is good. You won't dare call yourself a hero because that is letting the left hand know what the right is doing. You won't even think about a reward. But you will give full measure, pressed down, and flowing over, because your only interest is to benefit the other person, to make the adequate response.

The counselor, of course, must know the techniques of his calling and all about referrals. He must often chafe under the bureaucracy while doing the paper work, but in the midst of it all, he is the bearer of life. For guidance is much more than knowing the ropes; it is an act of love. There are no mechanical solutions in this business, as though by pulling the right strings you could adjust a personality to his environment. Adjustment is not a matter of tuning up the machine. Those who think it is—people-tinkerers, I would call them—have conceded the whole case to social and psychological determinism. They imagine that the cure for the disease is to treat the patient with a still more vicious form of the disease. But you cannot meet the challenge of determinism by conceding that its basic assumptions are correct, namely, that all human efforts and actions are the necessary product of antecedent conditions and causes, known or unknown, so that freedom becomes an illusion born of ignorance. If this were true, then man would be no better off than the animals whose actions are governed by instincts, drives, and appetites, and the greatest fools would be the saints and those secular heroes who died that others might have life. After all, why should we respect or honor them since they were not really free but moved by social and psychological pressures, all of which can be explained in terms of the hidden determinism of self-interest?

In view of this rather widespread philosophy, which has affected not only academic circles but many young people with scarcely more than a grammar school education, I have tried to indicate the importance of showing people that they are free. In order to do this, it is essential that they experience freedom by performing at least one completely unselfish act. And if they are to see that this is possible, there is no substitute for the Gospel of Christ communicated, not so much by preaching and teaching, as by living and doing. And it is here that the attitude and spirit of self-sacrifice of the counselor is so important.

I hope you will not be too disappointed to find that the philosopher whom you called in to speak to you on the philosophical roots of guidance has concluded by bringing in the Gospel. No doubt, this does need some justification. My answer is as follows: if it is legitimate for philosophers to examine and discuss the great moral and religious thinkers of antiquity, both in the East and West, why should they be forbidden to discuss the code and creed of every faith but one? Even if the New Testament is studied, not as divine revelation but as a profound moral document, it is still a challenge to naturalistic determinism.

Whether or not you admit that God is the author of the Bible, you will not find a better argument for universal brotherhood and the unity of man than the parable of the Good Samaritan. This story, as exemplifying what one's free response ought to be when a fellow human being is in need, speaks for itself. The same is true of the Sermon on the Mount. Whether or not Christianity is accepted as a supernatural religion, it still constitutes the great revolution in vindicating man's freedom. Nothing that has followed since, neither Spinoza, nor Kant, nor Hegel, nor Dewey, nor Freud has succeeded in dethroning Christian wisdom as the most challenging moral doctrine in history. For this reason, even as a philosopher, I felt obliged to appeal to this wisdom and to the humility, charity, and love that it teaches in order to give the hint of an answer to a problem in guidance which, after all, is rooted in philosophical presuppositions.

REFERENCES

Collins, James. *A history of modern European philosophy.* Milwaukee: Bruce Publishing Co., 1954.

Greeley, Andrew M. The new breed. *America.* May 28, 1964. Vol. 110.

Hampshire, Stuart. *Spinoza*. Baltimore: Pelican Books, 1953.
Kant, Immanuel. *Foundations of the metaphysics of morals*. New York: The Liberal Arts Press, 1959. Tr. by L. W. Beck.
Lewis, Jerry. *The Saturday Evening Post,* October 12, 1963.
Salinger, J. D. *The catcher in the rye*. Boston: Little, Brown, 1945.
Wheelis, Allen. *The quest for identity*. New York: W. W. Norton, 1958.

ADDITIONAL READING

Allport, G. *Becoming, basic considerations for a psychology of personality*. New Haven: Yale Univ. Press, 1955.
Beck, C. E. *Philosophical foundations of guidance*. Englewood Cliffs, N.J.: Prentice-Hall, 1963.
Berdiaev, N. *The destiny of man*. New York: Scribner, 1937.
Bingswanger, L. *Being in the world (selected papers)*. New York: Basic Books, 1963.
Buber, M. *Between man and man*. Boston: Beacon Press, 1955.
Buber, M. *I and thou*. New York: Scribner, 1958.
Castiello, J., S.J. *A humane psychology of education*. Chicago: Loyola, 1962 (reprint).
D'Arcy, M. C. *The mind and heart of love*. New York: (Meridian Book) H. Holt, 1945.
Dawson, C. *The crisis of western education*. New York: Sheed & Ward, 1961.
Dewey, J. *Democracy and education*. New York: Macmillan, 1916.
Donceel, J. F., S.J. *Philosophical psychology*. New York: Sheed & Ward, 1961 (2nd ed.).
Frankl, V. *The doctor and the soul, introduction to logotherapy*. New York: Knopf, 1955.
Frankl, V. *Man's search for meaning*. Boston: Beacon Press, 1963.
Gilson, E. (trans. L. K. Shook). *The Christian philosophy of Saint Thomas Aquinas*. New York: Random House, 1956.
Lapiere, R. *The Freudian ethic*. New York: Duell, Sloan, & Pearce, 1959.
Marcel, G. *Homo viator, introduction to the metaphysics of hope*. New York: Harper, 1962.
Maritain, J. *Education at the crossroads*. New Haven: Yale Univ. Press, 1943.
Maritain, J. (ed. D. Gallagher). *The education of man*. Garden City, N.Y.: Doubleday, 1962.
Misiak, H. *The philosophical roots of scientific psychology*. New York: Fordham U. Press, 1961.
Rogers, C. R. *On becoming a person*. Boston: Houghton Mifflin, 1961.
Royce, J. *Man and his nature, a philosophical psychology*. New York: McGraw-Hill, 1961.

Russell, B. *Education and the modern man.* New York: Norton, 1932.
Shinn, R. L. *The existentialist posture.* New York: The Association Press, 1959.
Sonnemann, U. *Existence and therapy, an introduction to phenomological psychology and existential analysis.* New York: Grune and Stratton, 1954.

Edward J. Sponga, S.J.

is provincial of the Maryland Province of the Society of Jesus. He received his A.B. at Georgetown University, completed theological studies at Woodstock College, and was awarded the Ph.D. degree at Fordham University. His academic experiences include high school teaching, teaching philosophy in college, dean of a graduate school and president of Woodstock College. He was president of Scranton University before holding his present post. He holds membership in the following professional organizations: the American Philosophical Association, the American Catholic Philosophical Association and the Jesuit Philosophical Association. He has participated in numerous national and international conferences in which he has discussed the integration of the data of the theologian with the work of the counselor.

Theology and Guidance

An important relationship between theology and guidance has been seen by those individuals who have sought in any way, theoretically or practically, to relate God's communications of Himself to mankind with man's own felt need for a satisfying understanding and acceptance of himself and society. Theology, even in its strictly formal sense of a scientific study of God, has always admitted the adjective "pastoral" to designate the relevancy of its doctrines to the good human life even on this earth.

It is true that theology and guidance have not always maintained a close friendship. At times the relevancy of the doctrines of theology to concrete personal attitudes and conduct has assumed a position inherent within dogmatic theology; at other times this relevancy has been relegated to a rather peripheral role. Such fluctuation has responded to the shifting emphasis in dogmatic theology itself in the history of Christianity. As theology veers excessively toward the refinement of rational elaboration and propositional clarity and logicality, pastoral theology assumes the role of an ancillary skill, useful in making the precepts of moral theology comprehensible and more acceptable to the individual penitent. In this theological climate, pastoral theology is concerned with leading the individual person to face squarely his obligations under the law of God. It seeks also by persuasion, enlightened hopefully by some basic understanding of the art and science of interpersonal relations, to help the individual to muster the necessary will power to overcome his feelings and to obey the rather categorically-defined precepts of God's will. On the other hand, as theology becomes more closely concerned with the actions and words of God as He revealed Himself in the dialogue of human history, using the language and images of the ordinary man, then pastoral theology becomes almost synonymous with theology as such.

Pope John XXIII said, when he convened the second Vatican Council, that he considered its aim to be pastoral rather than dogmatic. Partly as a result of this impetus we are witnessing today the shift in theology toward a closer relation with Scripture and biblical themes, with the liturgical life of the Church, and with the rejuvenated study of catechetical methods. In this climate, the lines between theology as a science and as "useful" for man's life (though such lines cannot totally disappear) are shading off. In this context, we become more aware that God's revelation of Himself can only be truly understood when man loves God in that dialogue with God which is man's daily effort to know and be himself. In this case, theology itself becomes, without ceasing to be scientific, more sensitive to all that is human, seeing this as the living link with God Who is Himself personal and Who became, in some always unexplainable way, one of us. In this view, nothing that is relevant to man and his universe is irrelevant to our understanding of God's revelation of Himself to us and of His guiding of men toward the fulfillment of the divine desire for us. Conversely, nothing that theology has to tell us about the living God and His dwelling in our midst is unrelated to man's ability to assess his own work and to promote his own well-being in time and in eternity.

Hence, it follows that the more a person engaged in guidance comprehends what theology in this fullest sense of the word has to offer, the more he will be alert to *all* the dimensions of the individual person and society which he is trying to aid. With a heightened alertness to all human dimensions, he will be able to guide, to suggest, to help his individual client to free himself so that the client can take fuller hold of his own life. Thus he would be able to assist his client to attain a more meaningful acceptance of his limitations and to a more purposeful effort to develop his true resources. And I do not hesitate to say, on the other hand, that the theologian who is not in active contact with the current developments in the understanding of the inner needs and workings of man and his universe as they are today, and who does not experience—at least to some degree—the way the human heart is striving for its meaning within the context of today's world, will soon find his theological understanding progressively shrinking into concepts and propositions with but minimal contact with the living personal God. And then, pastoral theology becomes some kind of theological jurisprudence.

THEIR COMMON ROOTS

Theology and guidance ultimately are pertinent and helpful to each other because their respective roots meet in the subsoil of the concrete existing human person. Although it is difficult, especially within a limited time, it seems imperative to make a boring into this subsoil in order to expose why it is that guidance will be as effective as it is aware of man's most fundamental potential and impulse.

The theologian insists that every human person who exists, be he Christian or anything else, is radically related in his total existential being and powers to God, Who created him, to Christ, in Whose Image he is made, and to the Divine Spirit, Whose life he must somehow possess. Certain conclusions follow from this theological premise which pertain in some way to every human person. Since he is totally a product and image of God, his Maker, and since God is, in His very Divine Being, love, then the human person is fundamentally constituted by love. Man is a person, that is, to the extent that he loves God, others, and himself in God. Man was first loved before he could love and thus he always remains. But man must take possession of his integral personality. He is not made totally without his own free embracing of what he is. This means that every individual whom you meet or try to guide has made, perhaps in some gradual and only obscurely conscious way, a choice about whom he would be. Ultimately, the choice was but one of two alternatives: he chose to be what God made him to be—a creature, totally dependent on a God Who gave him all as a gift, and not because of his own achievements. He chose, that is, to love this God, His loving Father, and therefore to love himself as one who has received all that he has. Or else, he rejected this and chose to be what he wanted to be, not beholden to any other Ultimate; he chose to orient all else and all others around himself. Such a radical position, talking about one's own meaning, is often not clearly expressed even to one's self, especially in the case of the option to be one's own god. Frequently, it is really the result of a refusal to make the choice to be what God made me to be. But this choice is of most fundamental importance in the making of every human being, and there is no real understanding of him, or truly effective helping of him unless one realizes this. The person who chooses to be what he alone decides, lives in an unreal world. If he is psychically strong, he can function ordinarily with success in a limited way. If not, he will have increasing recourse to means of escaping the self he refuses to accept, but cannot totally ignore.

Both the man who chooses to be what God made him to be and the one who rejects this, work out their respective choices in time. Man must win his personality and hence his freedom and he does this by living out his love—or choice—in daily fidelity in the most normal actions of human life. Each good action, that is, an action in accord with what one really is, frees a person of self-centeredness a bit more. On the other hand, every action aimed at the making of self god binds one a bit more to the world of unreality he is trying to fabricate. While a fundamental choice is much conditioned by the context of our individual lives and the influence of other persons, each person is ultimately guided by a great love—God or himself—and he uses all the circumstances of his life accordingly.

The theologian notes one other fundamental truth about the existential human person: every human person is born already in trouble; he is born a sinner. Original sin is a latent self-love. This means that every human being is born with an inclination toward the wrong option. It is here that the totality of his inherent nothingness and the total need of God is revealed. To be able to make the right fundamental choice of his own identity, man must receive another gift—another communication of God's love, this time manifested in God's own Son become man. When I receive this new power to choose what I really am, namely God's son, I am identified with Christ, God's Son, by divine nature. Only within this identity can I be what I really am. Such love is not rooted in or rising out of human love, but in the revealed mystery of the Divine Love of the Son for the Father. Therefore, it cannot be the subject of psychological experiments. It is the object of faith. But it exists and existentially it has everything to do with every human person seeking to be someone or seeking happiness or fulfillment or whatever it may be called, depending on the level at which this God—impulse is met.

Now it is quite obvious that not every human being is aware, with any sort of conscious knowledge, of this total existential reality of his person. And it also is obvious that a guidance counselor does not have to know or accept as a fact this theological picture of man to be of some effective worth in guiding. But my point is: whether the counselee or the counselor knows it or not, the facts are there and to the extent that each individual knows them and embraces them, to that extent he will embrace his total reality. But since this knowledge entails supernatural faith and since, by definition, this is a pure gift of God, not everyone possesses it or knows about it. But this does not affect each individual's ability to make his fundamental option according to the lights he has actually received. It is on the basis of his sincere individual lights that he will find his meaning or not. In making each one of us unique, God's love comes to each in the particular way that God chooses—not all receive the same gifts and the lot of all is not the same. Some have a psychological weakness not ascribable to their own fault. This may often hinder their obtaining much of a moral or religious sense; but they will still be constituted as persons accordingly as they choose, to the best of their lights, to be for Another—that is, for God—or totally, contrariwise, for themselves.

Hence, such theological truths are most essential for understanding man and his aspirations, needs, fears, anxieties, and hopes. While a guidance counselor does not have to know all these theological facts to help a person release his potentiality and be freed of crippling anxieties, no counselor can really be of true help unless he at least accepts as a *real possibility* the existence of a personal God of Love, Who interests Himself in man. If the counselor has supernatural faith and is thereby capable of understanding the full worth of the person he is seeking to aid, he can be even more effective; he can see his own work as intimately related to God's mercy and love and he can realize thus the true dignity of himself and his work. Such a counselor cannot help but infuse the techniques he learns with a sensitivity, a patience, a courage, a selflessness that are the marks of the true guidance role. While the theologically attuned guidance counselor may rarely refer explicitly to the theological facts, yet if he is aware of them he will spontaneously see the individual search for emotional balance, for inner peace and self-respect, for a fulfilling occupation, as the manifestations on the psychological level of a deeper force—namely, the impulse of the human spirit seeking its God, Who is Creator, Redeemer, Father, Life, Truth. True, no amount of psychological skill or of theological background will enable the counselor to compel a selfish person not to be selfish. But such knowledge may give a counselor power to allow a selfish person to experience, perhaps once in his life, the impact of a selfless act. This could remind the counselee of the God he has rejected or twisted into his own image.

WHAT THEOLOGY OFFERS TO GUIDANCE

I hope that I have given some notion of the common vocation of theology and guidance sown in the depths of the mystery of the human person and his freedom. Let me move now to the level of a more conscious relationship between theology and guidance.

Guidance is a broad term which needs some definition here so that we can pinpoint its lines of contact with theology. By the term guidance, I am referring in general to a process employing various techniques to assess the relative weaknesses and strengths of a given individual's temperament, character and personality. The purpose of guidance is, through the providing of pertinent information and counseling, to enable an individual to make realistic plans and decisions about his life. Guidance may be more specified as, for example, it may concern itself directly with plans and decisions about the pursuit of one's education or occupation or state in life, such as marriage. Or it may be aimed more directly at enabling the human being to function with a minimum of self-crippling and a maximum of the sense of achievement and self-fulfillment. Guidance, while it may not ordinarily concern itself explicitly with obtaining one's ultimate destiny, will be most realistic when such ultimate values are the underlying orienting forces which structure all plans and decision.

In the process of doing this work of appraisal, instructing, suggesting, listening, there are certain basic psychological forces and counter-forces within every human person, stemming from the deeper drive of which we have spoken previously, with which every counselor must reckon. I think we can best make our liaison between theology and guidance by isolating these more important psychological forces and indicating what theology may have to offer in reference to them.

These basic human needs which must be controlled and handled constructively in the process of achieving well-being may be categorized in various ways. In fact, they may all be seen as simply various facets of one primordial need to be loved and to love. However, it will help to see some of the various facets of this need as it expresses itself in relationship to certain basic, human, individual and social goods.

In making decisions, choosing a vocation, avocation, or just what one will do with himself today, a person operates both in terms of emotional impulses and in view, at least at times, of some felt and desired value. The counselor must seek to channel the emotional drive. This he will do partly by proposing values which are valid and capable of being desired in some active way by the counselee. Certainly, even if he were fully aware of the theological dimensions to all human needs, a counselor could hardly hope to guide most of his clients by proposing such theological values in any formal fashion. Yet it does help him to know these dimensions and, since they are there as part of reality—in fact, the most basic part—it will help the client if these values are incorporated into his decisions to the degree to which he is capable of embracing such values at the moment. This inculcating of such values may ordinarily be done in a very indirect way; ultimately, it must be done by a process of progressive revelation to the counselee of what he really wants when he makes any specific choice, or refuses to make a choice. The guidance counselor must be able to recognize the true aspirations of the human spirit, no matter how they may come to the surface—in symbolic, confused, even in self-defeating ways. If the counselor also has a sense of the God-reference within all such expressions of need and anxiety, he will give his own work of counseling a firm base and release later in many of his clients forces for good that the counselor himself may never come to know of.

I will now isolate four facets of human need and relate them to pertinent theological truths. It will not be by chance that the pertinent theological doctrines in each case will be found to be areas of current theological emphasis and new growth. This phenomenon will, in fact, lend support to my initial statements about the more existential human orientation going on in the "new" pastoral look in theology. It will also, to some degree, by implication answer our other question, namely: what impact, if any, are guidance and its allied skills and sciences having on theology?

The four human needs on which I will fasten my theological reflections are: (1) the need to be loved and to love; (2) the need for security; (3) the need for a sense of inherent worthwhileness about one's work; (4) the need for a sense of oneness of meaning and direction within all the diverse pursuits and goals of life.

The need to be loved and to love, as I indicated earlier, is most fundamental in man lying, even in its psychological form, close to the core of the human person as a free, unique agent. Man is constituted a person by the fact that he is first loved by God. Man is furthered in the process of putting on his personal identity by the fact that he is loved or not loved, loved much or loved little, by those around him from the first moment of his life. If he does not meet true love, a concern for him, that is, which puts a certain absolute quality to his well-being, then he will find it most difficult to love in turn. He needs the physical and especially the emotional support of others; without it, he cannot come to really love or accept himself. And he cannot, in consequence, come to love or accept the one who ultimately is responsible for his condition, namely God. Without this sense of being respected for who he is as a unique human person, he cannot feel security, he cannot really find any work in life of sustaining value, he cannot see himself as anything but a lonely atom in a hostile environment, in the face of which he has only the option of waging an endless and hopeless war, or succumbing to one or other of the reality-escaping mechanisms of his own psychological impulses.

Whatever immediate specific problem guidance may be seeking to deal with, the elements of the problem are ultimately functioning in a positive or negative way as they are felt to constitute or block the desire of the person to experience himself as the object of respect and concern and to be able in turn to find the ob-

137

ject of this own concern outside himself in the other. Usually this desire is unexpressed and even unconscious. The Catholic doctrine of grace as the gift of God to us, constituting us in a special relationship of friendship and filial love with Him, has always been a sustaining realization for all those who can truly grasp its significance. God, Who loved us in the very act of creating us, loved us in an even more intimate way—striving, as it were (to use our necessarily inadequate human expressions), to put us on a closer level of equality with him and thus to make us more inherently lovable. He has surrounded us with gifts; yet He awaits our acceptance of His gifts. The most radical psychological problems stem from the existential rejection by a human being of his basic status as totally a "receiver of gifts," the refusal, that is, to accept that one's total worth lies in the fact that one is loved by another, namely, by God. The person who has to pay back every gift he receives is manifesting a fundamental refusal to accept love in its essential gratuity.

Current trends in theological writing concerned with grace are, without in any way neglecting the objective aspect of grace, rather, emphasizing the personal encounter element entailed in this divine self-gift giving. This has traditionally been called God's indwelling in the spirit of the just man. Theological writing now is noting that the indwelling brings about in man's spirit a relationship not to the Godhead, but rather to each of the individual Divine Persons precisely insofar as they are Persons. This more personalistic view of the Divine indwelling has some obvious relation to satisfying human longings, especially the need to be loved, to be understood, to be the object of another's concern. This view of divine indwelling invites a person to realize that he lives in familiar union with the Father Who resides in his spirit as his Father, with the Son as his brother, and with the Holy Spirit as his confidential friend. A consciousness of this objectively real union of the Three Divine Persons with his own personality can, as it is truly appreciated through prayer and reflection, bring alive in an individual an unshakable conviction of truly being the object of divine concern and hence, inherently worthwhile in himself and capable of bestowing love and concern on others, a worthy gift given by him even when it is not accepted at times by others. With this realization, he rarely experiences a depressing loneliness for he lives in an ever constant presence of the Other, i.e., God, in His threefold personal reality. God is seen not as One giving graces as if they were things, but as giving Himself. Man will, of course, still need and desire the emotional support of other human beings. But with this new sense of his own worth because he is loved by a Supreme Love, he is conscious of an absolute dimension in his being. This sense will, in turn, free him so that he will spontaneously open himself to sincere and often warm, emotional response from others. A person who senses within himself what constitutes his true lovableness will, as an overflow of this inner satisfaction, be increasingly thoughtful and sensitive in his relation with others and this in turn will evoke from others the respect and concern which he needs.

The need for security is radical in all of us. Unless we can be at least relatively certain of our possession or attainment of various basic human goods, we cannot be but eaten up with inner anxieties. As long as one is insecure, he cannot afford to take a risk and without risks human life atrophies and dies. The impelling motive behind many choices in life is the desire to attain what will make us secure, be it knowledge, status, money, occupation, even the love of another person. We need to feel that we have the resources to weather any attack. Without security we cannot trust ourselves to others or even to ourselves. Social relationships become so many threats to the insecure person. Because he is afraid he will not risk the unknown, the new, the different, anything that savors of vulnerability to others. Hence, he cannot love and he makes himself most unlovable for his efforts to love assume the form of seeking to control and dominate. His very environment, which should support him and render him secure, is seen by him as a threat. Hence, he cannot work cooperatively with others.

St. Paul himself gave us the basis for what has been traditionally known in the Church as the Doctrine of the Mystical Body of Christ. This teaching views the collectivity of all those who accept Christ as constituting with Christ, as Head, an organic unity after the analogy of the human body. It is only in recent years that we have begun to savor this teaching with anything more than an intellectual assent. We are, for many reasons today, in a position where we need this doctrine to sustain us, to give us the sense of security which we are being denied because of many threatening pressures in the world in which we live. The profound study of this doctrine going on today has served to direct emphasis away from the merely external aspect of the Church and toward seeing it again as the ongoing life of Christ. We are repeating more frequently and with a growing awareness of its reality such phrases as "the Whole Christ," "Christ Suffering Today in His Members," "Encountering Christ in Dialogue with Others."

The doctrine of the Mystical Body meets the growing malaise of insecurity. This doctrine provides the individual, in proportion to his comprehension of it, with an unshakable foundation for security. It makes him "belong" in a way that is not dependent on the whims of individuals or of social structures. It unites in a most balanced way the fulfillment of two often opposing needs of the individual—the need to belong, to be part of a group, and the need to maintain one's own identity as an individual person. Most insecurity today is generated by the inability to fulfill both of these human needs to a proper degree. The image of the "organization man" reminds us of the fact that the rapidly advancing complexity and inter-involvement of our lives is making us at once more interdependent and mutually vulnerable. Yet we find it increasingly difficult to be an individual without the group. We resent the inroads of the group on our privacy and we resent the failure of the group to supplement our increasingly circumscribed individuality. A doctrine that enables us to see the advancing socialization of our lives as a beneficial, rather than a destructive, force is vitally necessary. Communism had its try but proved itself more effective only in the destruction of human freedom. Yet a doctrine is needed to redeem the inevitable social complexity of our lives. The person who can see today's world as the invitation to find his true identity and full individuality in the organic living unity effected and maintained by and in Christ has a kind of security that cannot be obtained in any other way. He sees himself as at once totally involved in the life of God going on within the human race and as meaningful precisely as a distinct, unique individual in that whole with his own unique possible contribution. With this assurance, he can suffer without an inwardly consuming fear and he can become involved with all, knowing that he will, in fact, be himself fulfilled thereby.

Closely allied to the need for security is the need for a sense of achieving something worthwhile in one's work. It is being said by some now that this sense is dying in men today. It is said that more and more people find nothing fulfilling in their work and are becoming increasingly able to function in some kind of neutral gear until their day's work is over. If this is true then an even more serious problem exists, namely, the need to restore the sense of the importance of one's work. Paradoxically, religion itself has been accused at times of not taking this world and the things of this life seriously enough. To the extent that this charge was true, it is for quite a different reason from the one underlying any modern tendency of men to find their work unimportant. In the former case, the value of the works of this life were underplayed not because they had no value but because they were not seen as inherently related to the more permanent values of the next life. Today's loss of a sense of the value of work springs from a loss of a sense of values entirely. Certainly the mature human being, as well as the person with a true religious outlook, finds the accomplishments of human effort, ingenuity, and cooperation meaningful in terms of authentic human values. This applies to the works of art as to the achievements of the sciences, philosophy and technology. In what one makes, he articulates and finds himself. He reveals himself to others and finds himself again in their response to his labor. If one does not achieve such expressions in his daily work day, he must find it in some other form.

The Church has always had a doctrine of the intrinsic value of work as man's cooperation with God in releasing and reveal-

141

ing the Divine Beauty, Power and Wisdom in this universe. I am sure that the genuinely religious person is thrilled with the possibility of seeing God "from a new angle" in the opening vistas of space travel. The Church has, by God's gift, always had a sacramental outlook—an outlook stemming from God's own assuming of material elements in the action of divinizing man. Reasons of polemics have caused theologians in the past to play up the divinely-guaranteed results of the valid use of these sacramental acts. The effort has been a tendency to play down the role of the recipient, making him appear largely as a passive receptacle into which grace is poured if he does not resist. Theologians now are recalling the active and personal involvement of the recipient. They are emphasizing the fact that his acts of faith, love and desire are necessary if the sacraments are to produce their complete and proper effect. Men are not sanctified or transformed in any way by inanimate things such as water, oil, etc., of themselves. The things, and the actions involving the use of things, are given transforming power only by divine desire and, in the case of the seven sacraments, by explicit divine institution. These material things and actions are meant to be the symbol, the unifying situation bringing together God and man through the mediation of material creation. Man has a basic need to do this. God has raised this need to a new level, making its fulfillment not only essential for man in his personal development as man, but transforming man in a higher sense—namely, divinizing him. Theologians, therefore, are today speaking more about the reception of the sacraments as a meeting or encounter with God, with the Three Persons as Persons. By viewing his reception of the sacraments in this light, man can do much to enhance the grace which the sacraments effect. Man is thus reminded of his responsibility in the development of the fullness of the life God offers him. He sees himself, then, not so much as an instrument used by God to release God's Image in this world and in others, but also as a God's helper in this work.

The sacraments also have a social character which is being re-emphasized today. Since the Church is a community, as said above, the transforming action of the sacraments affects her members not as isolated individuals only but also precisely as members, that is, as related to each other. This is especially true of the sacrament of the Holy Eucharist—the symbol and effective food creating Christ's life in all who receive Him. A bond of affinity is thus revealed between all creation and the Three Persons in the Divinity. Man's work, therefore, is seen to possess the inherent character of being able to reveal not only the qualities and forces of matter, not only the skill and genius of man himself, but the presence, power, beauty, wisdom and love of God Himself. A man with this realization will have a sense of the importance of all his work in the degree that it reveals the divine.

Finally, man suffers today from the devisive and disintegrating effect of being constantly subjected to manifold and diverse demands upon his time, energy and resources. Unless he has learned to pace himself, to husband his resources according to a realistic hierarchy of needs, he can quickly be caught up in a frenzied round of activity. Pressured by fears and uncertainties, he becomes insecure and his insecurity is not relieved by a sense of self-confidence and worthwhileness which his daily work should give him.

He is bombarded by the mass media with all kinds of distorted values. To protect himself from this maelstrom of conflicting theories and demands, man today may readily settle for the false security of the crowd. He then falls into the lockstep march of all those who are going nowhere together. Their security lies in the illusion that someone is directing this march and that that someone knows where all are going. But this sort of ostrich-like security breeds confusion and hopelessness in all those who are still capable of thinking, at least at times. Man needs today more than ever a sense of direction which also means a sense of unity of meaning within the many different things he must do. The man today who has a strong sense of direction, who is not seriously disturbed by obstacles, sudden changes and reversals stands out above the crowd. People seek him out, hoping to absorb from him some of his inner harmony. The man who is so integrated is also most productive in every way. His energy is not drained by inner, unresolved conflicts. I suppose with some people there is a certain mystique attached to being one of the drifting crowd. They imply that it is somehow not quite human to be sure of your goal and your general direction. A few chosen individuals may be able to find purpose in thus identifying themselves with purposelessness. It may be that they become living symbols of the character of modern man; if so, they do have a unifying purpose. But most men need to find a certain strand of consistent meaning in all that they do. They have to be able to step back from the moving stream at regular intervals and check their bearings against a sure point of reference.

The Church today has become increasingly sensitive of this need that men have for a principle of integration in their lives. The principle has, of course, always been there. But it has grown obscure as the action of worship became separated from the other actions of life. It is the people themselves who often, without realizing it, have been making their needs felt by their growing demand for a kind of worship that they can share in, actively and collectively. No one can escape the fact that most basically man is a worshipper, that is, one who recognizes and honors the Source of his being. Man feels the need to do this formally at times with actions that involve all his powers, including his body. He feels the need to experience his unity with others in this meaning and in this basically human action of worship. He is struggling to remove the barriers of disunity in his various ecumenical efforts. Besides this need for a formal expression of worship, man needs to experience a sense of unified orientation of all that he does toward the same goal—the worship of God in *all* things. There is ultimately no other universally valid meaning inherent in all man's actions and in the very existence of all creation. Hence, it is not surprising that an age most in need of unity and integration should turn to seek it in a developed sense of worship or in a liturgical sense. A liturgical view of life is an attitude of mind which sees in the Church's worship and pre-eminently in the Sacrifice of the Mass the "making holy" of all created things through their restoration to God via man. Formal liturgical actions provide the matrix for the experience of the rightness of this view. This in turn enables a person to sense the sacral dimension in everything he does. He becomes growingly aware that whether he eats or drinks, or teaches or studies, or works or plays, all that he does in accord with the moral law, is capable of being the vehicle of his honor and praise of the Maker and Father of all things. Such a conviction furnishes a person with a sense of dignity and self-respect bred of an inner awareness of the harmony of all things and his role as the one who reveals and directs this harmony. He senses that in everything he does he fulfills, in a very personal though most social manner, the purpose for which he is created—namely, to be a co-lover and a co-worshipper of God in company with God's Incarnate Son and His total body, the Church.

WHAT GUIDANCE OFFERS TO THEOLOGY

I hope that this rather sketchy summation of certain most active theological currents and their reference to the goals of guidance give some sense of the other aim of my paper, namely, to indicate any influence that guidance may have on theology. There is no need to stretch this point out. To what extent guidance and the allied fields are actually influencing theology today and to what extent both theology and guidance are under some same influence, rising up from the needs of modern man, would be difficult to spell out. I would only say that for various reasons of cultural, economic, political, social, and kindred character, man is more conscious of his need to be a full person with the maximum of freedom befitting his situation as a redeemed creature, a symbol-making being, a social being. He thus requires more than ever skills and sciences which enable him to plan and effectively work to achieve his inner fulfillment and harmony. Guidance is one of these aids he needs, and he needs a guidance more than ever alert to all the dimensions and forces and needs within his being. Man also needs more than ever a kind of theology that springs out of living, constant dialogue between himself and his God, Who is also personal. This means that not only concepts but also human affectivity must somehow be found to be essentially involved in the knowing and loving of God. Man's most immediate, ordinary entrance into understanding and loving a person is through his experience of this interpersonal relationship with all the joy and pain and discipline of selfishness that it demands. This means that man's approach to God must be more and more through the experienced dimension of human life and love. Thus we find theology concerning itself more and more with the deeper reality of freedom, of intersubjectivity, of affectivity, of community, of natural symbolism without, of course, denying at all the need for constant conceptual redefining and restating. It is precisely within these dimensions that theology and guidance meet, although they are working at different levels and different immediate goals. But briefly, whatever makes us more truly able to understand and guide man to valid human goods, makes us more capable of grasping man's true relation to God. And conversely, the more we fathom by thought, prayer, and labor the inner beauty, love and wisdom of the Divine Persons, the more we fathom the full dignity of man and afford him an unshakable basis for self-respect, security, human love and communal living, and the ability to work effectively toward worthy goals in life.

By way of conclusion I wish, without in any way taking back all that I have thus far said, to return and clarify some lines of division that my integrating approach might have somewhat obscured. I believe, as you must have gathered, that theology and guidance have much in common and much to share. I do not in any sense mean that the theologian as such should be, or automatically is, a good guidance counselor, nor that a guidance counselor must be at least a minor theologian. The two disciplines work at two different levels. And to forget this would render theology meaningless, for the essential purpose of theology is to unfold, as far as possible, the implications of God's revelation of Himself, whether this has any practical utility for human life or not. The purpose of theology is not primarily therapeutic nor practical for finding a satisfactory job or education. To seek to make it so would mean the end of theology, for it would mean that God's only worth would lie in what He can do to make us adjusted, happy, effective. So likewise, the guidance counselor would soon lose his job if he spent his time explaining theological implications to the questions brought him by his clients.

But thus having clarified the lines of distinction, let me close with a return to my general theme and perhaps, this is the aspect that needs most emphasis today. Theology will become sterile if it becomes unrelated to human life, for our God is a living God and His living is always a revealing of Himself. Hence, He cannot be known to the degree which He wishes unless we stay immersed in human life and this universe around us. Guidance, on the other hand, cannot totally prescind from the ultimate meaning and destiny of all men. Hence, while theological doctrines have no place as such in the vocabulary or techniques of guidance, nonetheless, theological dogmas do provide valid analogies for the guidance counselor to transpose into his own level of functioning. The more depth of comprehension he has of man's theological dimensions, the more he will be able to assess specific tensions of a given client, the more he will be able to suggest insights enabling the client to uncover what he really wants to do and become.

REFERENCES

Aumann, Jordan (O.P.). Religious life and modern needs. *Rev. for Relig.*, 1954, *13*, 169-78.

Bier, William C. (S.J.). Goals in pastoral counseling. *Pastoral Psych.*, 1959, *10*, 9.

DeLetter, Prudentius (S.J.). The encounter with God. *Thought,* Spring, 1961, *36*, 8ff.

Dolores, Sister Marian (S.N.J.M.). *Creative personality in religious life.* New York: Sheed & Ward, 1963.

Fransen, Pierre (S.J.). Toward a psychology of divine grace. *Cross Curr.,* Summer, 1958, 211-32.

Goldbrunner, Josef. *Holiness is wholeness.* New York: Pantheon, 1955.

Jackson, Gordon E. The pastoral counselor: His identity and work. *Jour. of Relig. and Health,* April, 1964, 250-70.

Jungmann, J. A. (S.J.). *A pastoral liturgy.* New York: Herder & Herder, 1961.

Maher, Trafford (S.J.). *Lest we build on sand.* St. Louis: The Catholic Hospital Association, 1963.

Meissner, William W. (S.J.). Prolegomena to a psychology of grace. *Jour. of Relig. and Health,* April, 1964, 209-40.

McDevitt, Augustine (O.F.M.). Current theological trends and the religious life. *Proceedings Second National Congress of Religious of the United States* (Men's section). Notre Dame, Indiana: University of Notre Dame Press, 1962.

O'Connell, Matthew (S.J.). The sacraments in theology today. *Thought,* 1961, *36,* 40-58.

Oraison, Marc. *Love or constraint: Some psychological aspects of religious education.* New York: P. J. Kenedy & Sons, 1959. Paperback edition, New York: Paulist Press, 1961.

Rahner, Karl (S.J.). *The Christian commitment: Esasys in pastoral theology.* New York: Sheed & Ward, 1963.

Schillebeeckx, E. (O.P.). *Christ the sacrament of the encounter with God.* New York: Sheed & Ward, 1963.

von Hildebrand, Dietrich. *Liturgy and personality.* New York: Longmans, Green, 1943.

ADDITIONAL READING

Allport, G. W. *The individual and his religion.* New York: Macmillan, 1950.

Cavanagh, J. R., M.D. *Fundamental pastoral counseling.* Milwaukee: Bruce, 1962.

Curran, C. A. *Counseling in Catholic life and education.* New York: Macmillan, 1952.

Danielou, J., S.J. *The Christian today.* New York: Desclee, 1960.

Donohue, J. W., S.J. *Christian maturity.* New York: Kenedy, 1955.

Evoy, J. J., S.J., and Christoph, V. F., S.J. *Personality development in the religious life.* New York: Sheed & Ward, 1963.

Greeley, A. *And young men shall see visions.* New York: Sheed & Ward, 1964.

Herberg, W. (ed.). *Four existentialist theologians.* Garden City, N.Y., Doubleday, 1958.

Lepp, I. *The psychology of loving.* Baltimore: Helicon, 1963.

Marian Dolores, Sister, S.N.J.M. *Creative personality in religious life.* New York: Sheed & Ward, 1963.

Merton, T. *Life and holiness.* New York: Herder & Herder, 1963.

Mouroux, J. *The Christian experience, an introduction to theology.* New York: Sheed & Ward, 1954.

Mouroux, J. *The meaning of man.* New York: Sheed & Ward, 1948.
Quoist, M. *The meaning of success.* Notre Dame, Ind.: Fides, 1962.
Raymond, Rev. M., O.C.S.O. *You.* Milwaukee: Bruce, 1957.
Schmaus, M. *The essence of Christianity.* Chicago: Scepter, 1961.
Snoeck, A., S.J. *Confession and pastoral psychology.* Westminster: Newman, 1961.

Thomas C. Hennessy, S.J., is Assistant Professor of Counselor Education, Fordham University. He received his Ph.D. at Fordham University and his experience includes high school teaching and nine years as a guidance counselor.

Walter Smet, S.J., is the Director of the government-sponsored Psycho-Medico-Social Center of Jesuit High Schools in Antwerp, Belgium. He obtained doctoral degrees in education and philosophy in Louvain and did post-doctoral work under Carl Rogers.

Sister Mary Thomas, O.P., is Guidance Coordinator of the Brooklyn, N.Y., diocesan high schools. Her Ph.D. was received at Fordham. She initiated and directed for several years the guidance services in one of the local high schools.

Benedict J. Trigani is a counselor at Monmouth Regional High School, New Shrewsbury, New Jersey. He was awarded a Ph.D. at Fordham University. Before assuming his present duties, he was a high school teacher.

Confidentiality—A Discussion

Fr. Hennessy: In the practical work of the guidance counselor there is an area that frequently calls for moral decisions. That is, where does confidentiality about the student begin and how far does it extend?

Sr. M. Thomas: It seems to me that there should be norms from moral theology here, for the use of counselors. I read recently in one of the professional journals that there is a growing concern among counselors that etiquette seems to be taking over for ethics in the area of confidentiality.

150

Question: Isn't there an almost necessary problem here? The counselor is supposed to work not only with students but also with teachers. He works with teachers as a means of helping the students. And that calls for an exchange of information, unless we picture the counselor as only receiving information and not giving any. And once the teacher says, "The guidance counselor and I were talking about you," many professionals think that you've lost any possible student relationship.

Fr. Hennessy: It seems to me that we must distinguish between the gossiping that goes on among professionals and professional consultation. Gossiping implies that the restraints of confidentiality have been disregarded, while professional consultation indicates adherence to a code of ethics. Perhaps the place and the conditions surrounding one's discussion of students has something to do with whether it is consultation or gossip.

Question: The counselor may just state that such-and-such a student saw him. Or he may mention the results of a group testing program. Surely these items are not really secrets. Would someone give a definition or a description of the type of secret that we're talking about?

Dr. Trigani: Perhaps a norm might be that you wouldn't be likely to learn the information without the student's telling you: friction at home, financial troubles, minor and senior brushes with the law that may perhaps involve the protection of Youthful Offender statutes. Then there is the possibility of many other items being regarded by the student as his secret: his hopes, perhaps even his occupational plans, his dating pattern, his religious activity or lack thereof. I heard of one young person who successfully kept his age a secret. The counselor sometimes has to judge that the student regards an item as secret. In other cases the student will be quite specific in asserting: "This is a secret."

Sr. M. Thomas: I believe that the type of secret you just mentioned is called by the moral theologians and ethnicians an "entrusted" secret. This is knowledge of something which one obtains on the implicit or explicit condition that it will be kept secret; professional secrets belong to this class.

Perhaps a great deal of the information which the counselor has may not really be secret at all. So with regard to much of the information there is no problem. If you give them non-confidential information and no more, this may be as much as they need.

Question: But if the teacher wishes information which definitely is confidential, and it is given by the counselor for the good of the student, isn't it true that then the information may be divulged?

Participant: Don't you think that the student has to give permission before this information is given? I believe that the student has to know and has to be consulted about this sharing of information.

Participant: The counselor can't always be guided by what the student is going to agree to or not agree to. The counselor's obligation is to use his own judgment. He may judge that he should not share the information itself with the teachers, but share the fact that there is information at hand. I think this is called sensitizing the teachers, alerting them to the fact that an individual has a problem but not giving the details. This way the over-all fact is shared, but the details are held in confidence.

Sr. M. Thomas: I agree. On the practical level you can't obtain the permission of the student before imparting information when it's done for his good. There wouldn't be any consulting in the school if you were obliged to get the student's approval. I think that this problem is related to the use of psychological tests. The principle is that you must have the free and informed consent of the counselee before giving the test. But to be assured of this the student would practically have to take it before he could give this "informed" consent. Nothing would happen in the school counselor's office if he were so hemmed in.

Fr. Hennessy: Probably because of my work as a priest, I'm very concerned and perhaps quite strict in my attitude toward confidentiality. I think that unless you have the permission of the individual student, that you should never discuss what went on in counseling. Sr. M. Thomas referred to the content of counseling as the source of "entrusted" secrets. That means that there are times when the obligation for secrecy no longer obtains. These occasions include the avoidance of serious harm to the common good (the nation, state, town, school), to another innocent party, to the counselor, or to the counselee himself. Note that what is involved is always a "grave misfortune," "serious injury," which presumably would happen very seldom. So the idea that after counseling with a student you take it upon yourself to explain the student's personal problems to a teacher is repugnant to me, unless I had the approval of the student. This is not so impractical as it seems. First of all, there aren't that many disclosures of a secret nature that are made to you and which you would judge useful to share with teachers. Second, if you think it may be advantageous to divulge this data, you will be likely to make this decision during the time of the disclosures by the student. You can ask his permission to share the information at that time, and you will usually find that he is pleased to grant it.

Once you take the strong position I outlined just now, certain advantages accrue to you as a counselor. Word gets around the school that you can tell him something and nobody else hears it unless you give prior approval. Furthermore, it takes care of many day-to-day decisions of the counselor such as, "Should I tell such-and-such to all of John's teachers?" It clarifies your primary work as a counselor of individual students.

Question: Doesn't this rather extreme view create other problems, especially vis-à-vis the faculty? I believe that the counselor is supposed to be working with the teachers, while he would seem to be operating independent of the teachers if he followed your view.

Fr. Hennessy: There certainly is a difficulty against my position here. It is possible that some individual teachers may feel hurt if they perceived the counselor as one who welcomes confidential information from teachers but who does not share his own knowledge of confidential information. However, two observations seem appropriate: first, the counselor does not have access to so much secret information in most schools that most of his time is spent in dealing with them; second, the overwhelming majority of teachers seem to respect the fact that a special degree of confidentiality is expected from the counselor. In general, they approve of this position, once it is explained to them. Of course, there's the rub—it must be explained, either privately or at teachers' meetings.

Participant: When I was in the armed services, I learned that the data which we thought was secret, including medical records, could be subpoenaed and brought out in open court. I became convinced that there were no real secrets in the armed services. Is there any analogy here with regard to the secrets that the counselor has access to in the schools?

Dr. Trigani: I think that there is a close analogy in the two settings. In the services it is really difficult for anyone to have access to the medical records except in the case of an official inquiry or a court martial. The counselor and the psychologist are also not free from the possibility of subpoena. This is a very serious theoretical problem for psychologists and counselors. The professional associations are striving to obtain professional immunity from the possibility of courtroom inquiries. As the situation exists now, in New York state at least, anything that the counselor writes about a student, even rough notes, is judged to be part of the school record and could be subpoenaed by the courts. Obviously, this happens in only very rare occasions.

Question: An investigator from the FBI or any government bureau comes to your school and asks about a student who was graduated a few years ago. Suppose the student got into considerable trouble in the school. What is your legal obligation in this case? Can the investigator insist on seeing your records about the individual?

Fr. Hennessy: Sometimes you hear stories of a young investigator insisting that he has the right to see such records. In fact, however, legal experts inform me that records of a confidential nature can be required of the school only when a subpoena is involved. So the investigator certainly has no right to see the records when he visits you in school. A related problem concerns your obligation to provide any information to the investigator. There is no legal obligation to do so. Even if the investigator asserts that your refusal to discuss the former student will be interpreted as a mark against him, the counselor should recognize this for what it is—a kind of blackmail. Certainly the investigator's job is made more difficult if you do not contribute to his file. He may have to work further in the case. But that should not influence the counselor, if he has decided that in a particular case the good of the country does not require his cooperation.

In most cases, of course, the good of the country does require the counselor's cooperation and even the yielding of secret information according to the norms which were stated earlier. Serious harm could come to the country if certain relevant information is not imparted.

It certainly would not be a good sign of patriotism and the discretion of the counselor and the school if there was a general policy of non-cooperation with government investigators. And I feel sure that wherever such a policy is followed the investigators would retaliate in some form or other.

Question: What about cooperating with a prospective employer when he asks for confidential data about a student.

Sr. M. Thomas: Most of the counselor's dealings with employers are of a non-confidential nature. However, when you come down to a particular job and a particular student, there are those other norms when there is no obligation to keep the secret, and in fact I wonder if the counselor isn't obliged to reveal some information to prospective employers. There's the firebug who set the locker room afire. He's applying for a part-time job in a lumber yard! There's the boy who was taken to court for tying up a child and burning its toes. He's applying for a job as a playground assistant. Serious harm to innocent parties and to the common good may come upon their securing these jobs. The counselor should reveal information to prevent their employment in this type of work.

However, in general, the counselor has an additional obligation in the school to secure employment for those who need it. So he must cooperate with prospective employers and make appropriate recommendations. Of course, he has the right to reveal only those secrets which are pertinent to the prospective employment. It usually doesn't endanger innocent parties or the common good that a student's parents are constantly bickering or are in debt. So if the counselor finds himself imparting this kind of information, he's not following the norms we're talking about, but is just gossiping.

Question: Can a counselor adopt a policy that he will never make out any recommendations to employers or to colleges to insure his not having any problem about confidentiality?

Fr. Smet: It strikes me that if he has the approval of his administrators he could adopt such a policy, but I doubt that it would be wise. Many decisions of this type flow from the job description. If the counselor in fact has obligations regarding the placement of students in employment or in advanced training, it does not seem to be prudent for him to cut himself off from an active role in the actual placement of these students. Furthermore, this type of non-judgment, non-reporting can become infectious. Teachers and other professional members of the staff also have problems about confidentiality and they too may decide that they cannot provide anyone, including the counselor, with the data they have at hand. And then we'd have a pretty kettle of fish!

Participant: I'm glad that the speakers so far have taken the position that in serious cases and for the reasons given counselors can go to the principal and others and explain a confidential situation. Otherwise some young people would feel that they have the right to tie your hands by confidentiality. And thereby a great deal of harm could come to the school, the family or to you. Yet in practical cases, I believe that even the experts find it hard to give decisions. Professional counseling and guidance is so relatively new that we're not sure what our exact responsibilities are and so we're not getting definite answers from the professional organizations or the moral theologians.

Sr. M. Thomas: The most that we have right now, I think, are some statements of ethical standards for our work. The American Psychological Association publishes *Ethical Standards for Psychologists,* which was revised in 1962. And the American Personnel and Guidance Association has a booklet on the subject, *Ethical Standards,* which is a reprint from the *Personnel and Guidance Journal* of October, 1961. The *Code of Ethics* of the National Education Association of the United States which was adopted in 1963 is also of some importance for us.

Fr. Hennessy: The APGA has been doing a considerable amount of work in revising its ethical standards, and I wish to urge all of our counselors to study carefully its published statements. Recently an inquiry was made at a guidance meeting to determine how many of the group even knew that the APGA had a statement about the ethics of the counselor. Although 75 percent of the meeting was composed of members of APGA only 40 percent of them even knew that their organization had a published code of ethics. Yet when the 1961 edition of the *Ethical Standards* was published a reprint copy was sent to each member of APGA. Most of them apparently didn't even look at the cover.

I think that it would benefit us to examine every phrase and word in the document of *Ethical Standards.* For example, I have objected to a part of Section D, #2 of this document, which states: "The member may withhold information or provide misinformation to subjects only when it is essential to the investigation and where he assumes responsibility for corrective action following the investigation."

An example of this sort of misinformation would be the assertion that a class was superior to or inferior to another class in some quality (when there was no basis in fact) in order to learn the effects of feelings of superiority or inferiority on the group. This is an example of what is called "the end

157

justifying the means," by which is meant, of course, a good end justifying an unjust means. In fact, I cannot see how this type of misinformation is anything but a lie, no matter who tells it, even if they are considered to be first-rate scholars. I submit that one reason for having a code of ethics is that even outstanding experimenters need guidance in the complicated labyrinth of the sophisticated practice of counseling.

Participant: It may interest the group to know that Fr. Lynch, S.J., has an article in *Theological Studies* on the subject of psychic privacy. His view is rather strict. He examines the notion of the general good, the good of an institution or of a school, and the good of the profession, versus the good of the individual. He believes that in many cases these two opposing "goods" cancel each other out and that as a result it would be a very rare case in which one is justified in revealing a secret because of the need of protecting society, or an institution.

Question: In many schools the counselor is a priest. Does this create a special difficulty vis-à-vis confidentiality?

Fr. Smet: Such a priest has a very complex role. We must distinguish between his role as counselor-educator and his role as a priest. At times the priest who is the school counselor is strictly an educator. He works on a team of educators and as such he must share in common with other professionals the information which he has received as an educator. I believe that the priest who is a school counselor must be aware of his function as a member of the educators' team. Otherwise he may not be building up the morale of the group, but may be subtly undermining it.

Fr. Hennessy: I think that the solution to this problem revolves around the decision which ultimately must be made concerning the exact role of the counselor. Granted that his work primarily centers upon the individual, is he a member of the administration or of the teaching staff? Or is he somewhere in between, with special relationships to each of these other groups?

Question: I wonder if there isn't some danger, even physical danger, latent in the great stress on the secret nature of some information? For example, people talk about the importance of keeping secrets about students for fear that the student may be damaged or misjudged in some way. But I as a teacher may be assaulted, ultimately, because I didn't know that a particular student had a psychological problem. It will provide me with little consolation if later on a member of the guidance staff tells me, "Oh yes, we know that he's likely to explode that way. We can't get him the help he needs."

Sr. M. Thomas: I believe that you have given a good illustration of a case in which the counselor is not held to confidentiality regarding a student's problem. Earlier mention was made of situations in which one is not held to keep a secret. One of these situations involved injury to a third innocent party or group. I believe that anyone whose work brings him close to such an individual has the right to be warned about him. Certainly the teachers who deal with him have such a right. What about the students in the same classroom? Usually they don't need any warning about this type of individual because they will take their cue in dealing with him from the faculty. In individual cases where danger seems to exist for someone who becomes quite antagonistic or quite close to such a maladjusted child, the teacher could warn him to keep his distance, but without giving reasons.

Question: Should this information, or "warning" about prospectively dangerous students be taken care of by the counselor or by the administration?

Fr. Hennessy: It seems to me that when the counselor concludes, after careful consideration, that his obligation for confidentiality does not exist in a particular case, he must normally go to the administration for the next step. The administration may decide to inform the proper teachers about the situation, or they may deem it best to refer the child to other agencies, if this is not done routinely. In many cases the administration would request the counselor to implement the decisions made in their consultation, but the counselor would then be operating as a special agent of the administration in this case.

Question: The decisions then lie at the counselor's whim for initiating action. In my own school there have been at least two cases where the guidance department refused to act and there were serious repercussions as a result. So I don't trust our guidance department and would like to see that copies of all confidential information went both to the guidance staff and to the administration.

Dr. Trigani: Perhaps the staff of the guidance department which you are speaking of has not received training in the specialized work of the counselor. I believe that most counselors who are trained will give serious, professional consideration to the information which is made available to them. Naturally, among trained counselors some will still be inclined toward caution and non-referral, while others might perhaps rush too hastily to the administration about a particular case. I see no need for duplicate copies of confidential material where you have a trained staff. And if the administration does demand duplicates of this type of information it will downgrade and demoralize the guidance staff.

Question: When we are talking of confidential information are we forgetting the cumulative record? The accrediting agencies, such as the Middle States, urge that all the professional members of the staff have access to the cumulative file on all the students. Will some of the secret information that we're talking about be in the cumulative file?

Sr. M. Thomas: What we're talking about would not be in the cumulative file. Besides the objective data in the cumulative record, which contains aptitude test reports, school grades, questionnaire information, summaries of anecdotal records and rating scale reports by teachers, an entirely different locked file usually exists in the guidance department. It contains the classified information we are talking about. There may be little that is truly confidential about the vast majority of students. But we are really talking about the secrets of the minority.

Question: What becomes of that file? Is it a file that really belongs to the counselor and which he can destroy when, for instance, he is transferred to another school? Does he destroy it when the student is graduated or some interval later?

Fr. Hennessy: Practices differ. However, I believe that this type of file is one which belongs to the counselor himself. If he is transferred, he can destroy it, or even bring it with him. This particular record perhaps cannot be properly interpreted by another. There was a unique relationship that existed, and in view of that, the young person sought help from this particular counselor. Perhaps he made revelations that he made to no other living person. Of course, one could argue the other way and say that the student saw the counselor only as the instrument of the school and that the record should stay with the department. While I do not accept the latter view, I can see that it is defensible, particularly in very large guidance departments where unfortunately many counselors regard themselves as but a cog in the works.

Question: How long should the counselor or the department keep these confidential files?

Dr. Trigani: Of course, we all accept the fact that the school is obliged to keep its records of the grades of students indefinitely. Regarding the keeping of the guidance confidential file, many counselors make a cleanup operation of students who were graduated for four years. The *Federal Register* of The National Archives publishes (latest edition, March 5, 1964) a "Guide to Record Retention Requirements." I think that it is pertinent to note that in case after case the different federal departments are not required to keep records beyond four years, and many have only a two or three year requirement. Of course, some records must be retained indefinitely.

Participant: I know of an eminently successful school counselor whose view of his function and role is quite different from that described here. He makes it known to the students that he is a school official, primarily. He tells them that what they tell him may be used against them and that if they want to come and talk to him about their difficulties, they must accept these conditions. His view towards secrecy is different from that of this group. But he has no lack of counselees because

161

the students know that he has their interest and that of the school at heart. They know that he's a perfect gentleman in his relationships with them. But there is an understanding that if they wish to discuss something that they wish to be kept secret, they should seek out someone else, not the counselor.

Fr. Hennessy: You observed that this counselor has different notions about his role and function. Apparently the administration in the school shares his views. However, if titles mean anything I would not like to hear him called a counselor since his role and function seems to be quite different from practices followed in most schools in the country. One wonders how closely his description of his work would coincide with that presented by the American School Counselor Association in its Statement of Policy for Secondary School Counselors (February, 1964).

When counselors meet these days, it often happens that their informal discussions pertain to their ethical practices. I believe that this tendency is a sign not only of the high moral level of these practitioners but also a vindication of counselors' claims to professional status. The professional person has, among his many skills and commitments, a deep concern for the uprightness of his conduct and his associates' conduct. There is not only a great deal of interest in the ethics of counselors but also much disagreement on this topic. The confusion flows from two main sources: lack of agreement on the exact role and function of the counselor, and a solid philosophical basis on which ethical principles of professional conduct should be based. The American School Counselors Association in the document which I just mentioned has done landmark work toward providing a basis for consensus about the role and function of the school counselor. With regard to the philosophical foundation for the consideration of the counselor's ethics, perhaps we must await symposia and high level conferences between the philosophers and counselors. Meantime, we counselors should become members of committees and study groups; some groups could spend time looking into the contributions of the "special ethics" of philosophical writers; others could be collecting data on the problems which counselors face in their practice, and in analyzing these data. When these well prepared groups meet with competent authorities in the field of ethics and counseling, answers to the problems which vex us today should be forthcoming.

The suggestion has been made that a special course be required of all prospective teachers and professional staff members in the schools. It would be entitled "Professional Problems in the Schools." One of the major segments of the course would be concerned with the understanding of the ethical principles of professional members of the teaching profession. This would be a step forward.

371.42
G94

Date Due

74749
